Floyd's
Thai Food

Floyd's
Thai Food

Keith Floyd

This book is dedicated to the memory of Khun Akorn

My thanks to:
The Intercontinental Hotel, Bangkok
Pakistan International Airways
The directors and staff of the Burasari Hotel, Phuket
My long-suffering editor Barbara Dixon
My wife Tess (thank God she knows how to use a laptop!)

With thanks to Nirun Jirapermpoon
and the Siam Royal Orchid restaurant
367 Uxbridge Road, London W3
for their help with translation

First published in 2006 by Collins
an imprint of
HarperCollins Publishers
77–85 Fulham Palace Road
London W6 8JB

www.collins.co.uk

Book produced for Collins by Essential Works Ltd
Editor: Barbara Dixon
Designer: Mark Stevens
Location photographer: Tony Hanscomb
Studio food photographer: Michelle Garrett
Cover photographer: Tony Hanscomb
Home Economist: Carole Handslip
Indexer: Hazel Bell

For Collins
Commissioning Editor: Myles Archibald
Production: Chris Gurney

Food photographs: (a = above, b = below, l = left, r = right, c = centre,
t = top)
39 cr; 44; 56; 58 tr; 60 c; 63; 67; 69 bt; 70; 76; 77; 83 tl; 84 c; 86–7;
90–91; 101; 108 tl; 110 c; 112; 114–115; 119; 124 tl; 126 c; 127 l;
133 b; 138–9; 160 tl; 161 tr; 162 c; 166–7; 176–7; 186

ISBN-10: 0 00 721 349 2
ISBN-13: 9 78 0 00 721349 8

Printed and bound by Butler and Tanner, Frome, Somerset, UK

Contents

Introduction

Introduction

The charm of Thailand

On this early Bangkok morning, the waiter brings me a bowl of plump, duck red Thai curry. I am drinking apple juice, it is six o'clock in the morning and yet the Intercontinental Hotel, where I am staying for free, is buzzing. Multilingual businessmen are eating with one hand while the other clamps their mobile phones to their ears. If you suffer from a hangover or jetlag, there is nothing better than this exquisite spicy food I am eating. My very good friends at Pakistan International Airways kindly flew me to Bangkok, but by the global scenic route (of course, I am not complaining because the flight was free – thank you, PIA) and, I must say, the in-flight Pakistani food is delicious. The reason I am wrecked at breakfast time like a wet sack of rice is because I flew from Heathrow to Lahore, from Lahore to Islamabad, from Islamabad to Hong Kong and Hong Kong to Bangkok and did not sleep a wink.

My driver, Pata, is waiting to take me away on this Sunday morning to the huge market where I will have another breakfast, this time of succulent, ripe mango and creamy sticky rice. A hawker, standing behind his mobile kitchen, built on an elaborate tricycle, laughs with charming disbelief when I request

Below left to right *A superb meal aboard Pakistan International Airways. Naheed Tabassum, a charming member of the crew. My good friend Mr John Nielsen of the Intercontinental Hotel, Bangkok.*
Opposite *Street food at Chatuchak Market, Bangkok.*

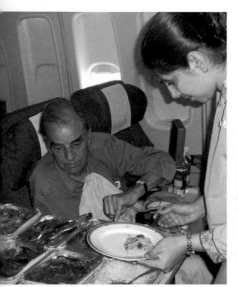

Opposite top to bottom *Grilling sticky rice and shrimp in banana leaves at Chatuchak Market. Luscious tropical fruit at the market.*
Above *Coconut juice is very refreshing in the heat of Bangkok.*

crushed, dried chillies to be sprinkled on my mango. That, washed down with the milk from a freshly decapitated coconut, has brought me and the morning back to life. For four hours I walk up and down the crowded stalls, while my photographer is taking pictures.

It is the rainy season and the humidity and temperature are insupportable. However, the charm of Thailand is washing over me like soft rain and it is funny to think that fifteen or sixteen years ago I was sitting in a hotel eating breakfast, but that time in Newcastle. We were about to film a BBC programme called 'Far Flung Floyd' and were due to go to Thailand. The general manager of the Gosforth Park Hotel told me I would enjoy meeting Thai hotelier Khun Akorn and his wife Chompanut. I asked him how he knew more about my life and my work than I. Enigmatically he said, 'Wait and see' and lit a cigar and swept out of the room.

I must point out that at that time, Akorn owned the largest hotel chain in Thailand, an empire that stretched from virtually the borders of Burma to the enchanting island of Samui. Akorn is sadly no longer with us, but because of him, and indeed his wife and his staff, every door in the country was opened to us during our filming. In his philosophical and altruistic way, Akorn wanted no

Opposite *These grilled sticky rice in banana leaf rolls are jolly good.*
Above *The wonderful beaches of the island of Phuket, getting back to normal after the Tsunami.*

commercial credit for what he did. He didn't want his hotel logos to appear on camera, he just wanted to assist us to show that Thailand is a magical destination. I frequently stayed with Akorn on Samui and, over a bottle of Black Label, we would talk of food and wine and Buddhism, while he puffed on an aromatic cigar as the waves lapped onto the nearby beach. I dedicate this book to him and his family.

So, here I am again, and now we've travelled to Phuket, where I'm having breakfast once again. Believe you me, breakfast is a very important meal in my life, because you never know the events that may unfold throughout the rest of the day. I am sharing my breakfast with Mr and Mrs Minah. They are sitting in the hanging basket of orchids just above my head by the pool, chirping happily here in the charming Burasari Hotel, where we are staying. From time to time, they hop onto the table for a few grains of rice or another sugar cube. I am eating boiled rice soup and pieces of roast pork, lashed with chillies, chopped spring onions and fresh coriander. It is hot, but I am feeling good.

Above left to right *A chance to chill out in Phuket – Pearl Island is in the background. Believe it or not, I'm drinking tea. These fish are so spanking fresh.*
Opposite *A wonderful array of Thai pancakes at the Damnoen-Saduak floating market in Bangkok.*

After breakfast, our hosts at the hotel, the managing director, a charming lady called Khun Lilly, the general manager, Mike, and the food and beverage director, Mark, take us on a gentle tour around the island.

Phuket was badly hit by the Tsunami of 2004, but apart from the emotional scars, it is pretty much back on track. The hotels are back in business, the great little tumbledown beach restaurants are back in business and, of course, the shopping areas are throbbing with people. There are some wonderful beaches, but if you want to get away from the crowds, you can go up into the richly wooded hills or take a long-tail boat to one of the many tranquil little islands that seem to float in clear, turquoise water – so clear that you can see the shoals of multi-coloured fish dancing around close by.

We stopped for lunch at a beach restaurant that Mike knew well and had some spicy, tangy salads – virtually the signature dish of Southern Thailand, the fiery prawn soup Tom yam goong and spanking fresh bream, dorade and other fishes simply grilled over charcoal by smiling, busy, cheerful ladies. It is too hot to drink wine, particularly in the daytime, so recommended drinks are – and this is what the locals have – freshly squeezed lime juice and soda, ice-cold Thai beer, or green tea (although many Thai people favour very watery whisky).

We sat on the beach under a banana leaf-thatched roof and watched the long-tail boats hurtling by and fishermen coming back with their catch to go and unload it against picturesque wooden piers.

The following day we flew back to Bangkok and checked into the Intercontinental Hotel, before taking an air-conditioned (essential) car ride

down to Bangkok's famous floating market. This is a complex of canals with pretty houses built on their edges, where you can take boat rides in cigar-shaped, traditional Thai punts, paddled gently through this labyrinth of waterways by smiling ladies. Tied alongside the main landing stage are dozens of these charming little boats, each with a lady in it, sitting cross-legged, selling their freshly picked produce – all kinds of greenery, lemons, limes and other fruits. Some are making delightful little Thai sweets, or stir-frying noodles, or grilling racks of prawns and small fish.

From there we move to the curiously named 'Floating vineyards', which are about 30 km outside the city and which take hours to get to because the Bangkok traffic is appalling. Since there is so much water available, these vines are planted on little raised, rectangular islands and they are irrigated twice a day by the simple expedient of a sluice gate. Hitherto, I had not known that Thai wine was produced in Thailand and, although quite expensive, it was jolly good.

Back to Bangkok and we hurtle around as many restaurants as possible to check out what is happening in this big city. Then, after a sightseeing tour, at lightning speed, of the incredible golden Royal Grand Palace, we get back, exhausted but happy, to the air-conditioned freshness of the hotel. We had been on the go for twelve hours this particular day and, after a shower and change of clothes, I sank happily into the comfortable bar and, as is the Thai custom, had a refreshing Johnny Walker Black Label with lots and lots of iced water.

Opposite top to bottom *A painted lady noodle seller of Damnoen-Saduak floating market. The Siam winery vineyard.*
Below left to right *It might be a precarious way of checking the grapes, but the end product gets my approval.*

Above *The stunning Royal Grand Palace, Bangkok.*
Opposite *I rustled up this plate of refreshing papaya salad with my old friend Marcel Nosari, executive chef of the Intercontinental Hotel.*

To my amazement, I saw a chef walking towards me in his immaculate whites and white clogs and, my goodness me, it was an old friend of mine, Marcel Nosari, now the executive chef of the hotel and trying to control 600 cooks, perish the thought! It was an invaluable meeting because he had just opened, in stark contrast to the beach bars and street vendors' chariots, a light, airy and exquisite Thai restaurant in the hotel, called the 'Charm Thai'. This served modernized and stylishly presented food, which I thoroughly enjoyed, but because my assistant Adrian cannot take spicy food of any kind, I managed to get special dispensation for him to have a fine steak, fresh vegetables and potatoes. I had a delicious deep-fried fish with chilli and cucumber sauce, followed by a spicy papaya salad and then a relatively hot yellow beef curry. The meal was finished by a sour tamarind sorbet and it was time for bed.

The next day, we took a terrifyingly fast, bouncing, long-tailed boat ride up the river past rickety little shacks standing perilously on stilts, and past the wats, all the while Tony the photographer shooting away like mad.

Opposite top to bottom *A trip down the Chao Phraya River, Bangkok. The bananas are creamy and cheap.* Above left to right *The colourful Chao Phraya riverbank. Scenes from Klong Toey Market, Bangkok.*

The city streets were heaving with stalls, food hawkers, errand boys carrying huge sacks of rice on their heads, women with huge wicker baskets filled with fruit and vegetables, open-air butchers, and fresh chickens crowded into igloo-shaped bamboo cages. But, Mark and Mike say it is time for us to go back to Phuket. We had to fly back there to meet the architects and designers who, I hope, are going to follow my suggestions for the creation of Floyd's Restaurant at the Burasari Hotel in Patong. We spent three days poring over plans, discussing menus and staff requirements, and although it is hard work starting any kind of enterprise like that (especially when you have to be *au fait* with Thai time), if you approach it gently as, by the way, everything that you do in Thailand should be approached, you will see why one smile makes two.

Keith Floyd
Burasari Hotel
Patong
Phuket
Thailand

2005

Tastes and tools of the Thai trade

Thailand is a magical and exotic country formerly known as Siam, with a famed royal family who endure and are adored by the Thais to this day, and I have been very lucky to have travelled north, south, east and west since I first went there in 1984. Thailand was never invaded or colonized by a European power. It is true there were skirmishes with Burma, but in the grand picture they are, today, completely insignificant. More important, though, are the gastronomic invasions that have taken place, which the Thais have welcomed, embraced and fused into their own rich, culinary heritage.

In Thai cuisine you will find the influences of Laos, Cambodia, Burma, Malaysia and, of course, China. But perhaps the most significant invasion came not from the region but from South America when, in the sixteenth century, Portuguese merchant men introduced to Thailand the signature taste of chillies.

Chillies and Thai cooking are symbiotic. From the explosively dynamite hot, tiny bird's eye chillies, right through the gamut of this exquisite vegetable to large peppers, green, yellow and red, chillies are extremely important to Thai cooking, and make vibrant displays in huge wicker baskets all over the country. Whether chopped fresh and popped into dishes or compounded into pastes, they are indispensable. Another vital ingredient is fish sauce, which is used throughout South East Asia instead of salt. Tiny fish, often anchovies, are laid

Below left to right *Red chilli paste is available ready-made from the markets. Juicy, aromatic limes. Local honey.*
Opposite *The Thais just can't get enough fresh and dried chillies.*

กะปิอย่างดี 60.-

out on the beach in their thousands and allowed to dry before being put into vats and left to ferment; incidentally, the Romans had a similar sauce that was called liquamen.

The explosive tastes of Thai food are also enhanced by the citric and sour flavours provided by lime juice, lemon grass, kaffir lime leaves and tamarind, and are then softened with either coconut water or coconut milk and the indispensable masses of fresh basil, mint and coriander – just loosely ripped up and chucked onto the top of any dish, they give a crunchy freshness and combat the fiery tastes.

In the north and north-west of Thailand, on the Burmese border, in the lush forests and jungles of places like Mae Hong Son and Chiang Mai, where wonderful rivers flow and working elephants bathe, you will find fiercely hot curries and salads. Even in the twenty-first century, the lore of the hunter-gatherer is reflected in the leaves and vegetables that are used for these salads – very often served with a warm dressing of chillies, fish sauce, palm sugar and lime juice – and in the very distinctive cooking of this region. Obviously, Bangkok, an international city, will cook, display and sell the delights of the whole country and, of course, the dreaded McDonald's, Pizza Hut and all the other appalling effects of American gastronomic imperialism.

As you progress south towards Malaysia, you will, as you do in Kerala in southern India, enter the world and the land of the coconut – so important in

Opposite *Bowls of fermented fish at Klong Toey Market.*
Below left to right *A few of the many vegetables used in Thai cookery. Preparing palm sugar. Coconuts awaiting collection by boat at the Damnoen-Saduak floating market.*

the rich, creamy, spicy, subtle, fragrant curries and the delicate, but deliciously sweet puddings.

In this slender volume, I am saddened that I do not have the space to eulogise at length over the subtleties and fundamentals of Thai cooking, so here, in a plain and straightforward way, are some brief, but important guidelines:

Basic utensils

Since in Thailand most of the cooking is done in huge aluminium vats over charcoal-fired barbeques, or in woks, or even, such as is the case with the famous sticky rice, cooked in bamboo tubes about 7.5 cm/3 inches in diameter (or baskets) over a low charcoal fire, it is going to be quite difficult, in our highly sophisticated Western kitchens, to replicate the amazing flavours that these simple heat sources create.

Since a lot of Thai cooking is done in woks, it is good to have a high-flamed gas stove, or, indeed, a powerful bottled-gas camping stove – you can cook outside when it is not raining. You will need a couple of woks, a small one and a

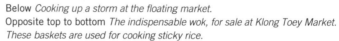

Below *Cooking up a storm at the floating market.*
Opposite top to bottom *The indispensable wok, for sale at Klong Toey Market.*
These baskets are used for cooking sticky rice.

Opposite top to bottom *Sticky rice for sale, alongside wooden pestles and mortars. The chopping boards are sturdy and need to be to withstand all the use they're put to.* Above left to right *Unidentified frying objects. The colours and shapes of turned wood are very attractive. Charcoal-fired cooking stoves.*

large one. If you have an electric cooker, buy flat-bottomed woks; if you have a fiery gas cooker, buy round-bottomed woks. You need a large pan for deep-fat frying, with a wire basket for straining. You need a couple of large bamboo steamers with lids and a suitably large pan the same size as the steamer so that it can sit on top of the boiling water. I do think an electric rice cooker is a really brilliant idea. Not only does it mean you will cook rice perfectly every time, but the rice will stay hot without spoiling for up to a couple of hours, and since the essence of Thai cooking is rice placed in the centre of the table, while everything else is just an accompaniment, this means that you can serve a small portion of rice time after time with each successive dish. For the serious-minded and those with ample time, a large, heavy pestle and mortar is *de rigueur* for preparing your pastes and salads. For those with less time, invest in an electric food processor. You will need sensible tongs to turn and lift the food; you will need wooden spoons or spatulas for stir-frying; a set of very sharp knives, and some substantial chopping boards. Should you find yourself on holiday in Thailand, you will notice in the markets that their chopping boards are mostly circular and cut from the trunk of a tree, upon which they deftly chop everything from chickens to vegetables with an extremely sharp cleaver – not for them a posey little knife rack filled with blunt knives acquired from some readers' offer in a magazine.

Ingredients

The Thais relish virtually every kind of green vegetable that there is, from Morning Glory, which is a form of lily pad, through to long **green beans** called

Above left to right *Galangal or Thai ginger. Krachai, a relative of ginger root, but milder than ginger or galangal. Lemon grass.*
Opposite *Not for the Thais mean little bunches of spring onions from the supermarket. Their leaves and herbs are super-fresh.*

Snake Beans. They can be between 30, 38 or 45 cm/12, 15 or 18 inches long. If you can find them, well and good, but I have substituted them with French green beans, a.k.a. haricot vert, which need to be topped and tailed and cut according to the recipe. They are a very good alternative.

Where recipes call for **shallots** or **onions**, please use red shallots and red onions.

Many Thai dishes require some **sugar**. Unless otherwise stated, this should be palm sugar or soft Demerara (or soft light brown sugar).

The basic **dark green leaves** used in Thai cooking are known as Chinese kale. In good Asian stores this is known as Gai larn. For ease of accessibility, I have substituted pak choi or choi sum. You could, of course, also use spinach.

Thais favour **galangal** over fresh root ginger because it is slightly sweet and more tender than ginger, but either can be used. Another great favourite, and member of the ginger family, is fresh **turmeric root**, a little yellow-ochre knobbly root about the size of your little finger. You might find this in good Asian stores.

When using **lemon grass**, remove the outer leaves and use the bottom 15 cm/6 inches of the stalk (or the white part only as specified). If you can't get lemon grass, use dried lemon grass (add a little extra for flavour), or the zest of 1 lemon (zest from 1 lemon = 2 stalks lemon grass).

An essential ingredient for cooking Thai food is **kaffir lime leaves**. However, if you can't obtain them, 1 tablespoon lime or lemon zest = c.6 kaffir lime leaves. If you are substituting dried leaves for fresh, they are much less flavourful, so use twice as many as the recipe calls for and, if possible, add dried leaves to the recipe earlier than you would fresh in order to extract the maximum amount of flavour.

Green curries, in particular, benefit from a few **fresh green peppercorns**; however, if they are difficult to find, buy green peppercorns pickled in brine, rinse them well and drain them. They make a fair substitute. The ones from Madagascar are particularly good.

Most Thai curries use **baby aubergines** the size of a large pea. They may be difficult to source outside of London, Manchester, Bradford and Leeds and other large cities, although you may find them frozen. If you are unable to find them buy small aubergines, cut them into 1 cm/½ inch cubes and leave the skin on.

Where **white vinegar** is required, try to buy first a) white coconut vinegar, b) rice vinegar, or c) white wine vinegar.

For **frying oils**, use coconut oil for stir-frying, if possible, and good-quality vegetable, corn or sunflower oil for deep-frying.

Thai curries differ dramatically from Indian ones. The Indian kitchen largely uses dried and often toasted spices. The Thai kitchen uses fresh herbs and spices, often toasted, to make a 'wet' curry paste. Thai curries can be severely hot, so take care with the chillies, especially the small bird's eye chillies. These tiny little things are absolute dynamite. As a rule of thumb, the seeds are the hottest part of the chilli and the pith the next hottest, and most chillies are fairly mild if these elements are removed – I leave it to you.

Let's put **Thai curry paste** on the line! Are you blender-lazy or pestle-proud? Traditionally, Thai curry pastes are made with a pestle and mortar. The ingredients are added gradually in the given order, starting from the hardest and the driest to the softest and the wettest, with each being reduced to a pulp before the next is added. As the ingredients are pounded, they release their fragrance and the balance of the paste can be sensed in the aroma and can be adjusted

Below *What these pineapples lack in size they make up for in sweetness.*
Opposite top to bottom *Pounding the spices for a curry paste at the Intercontinental Hotel. These mixed nuts are sold ready-chopped.*

Opposite *A trader prepares her wares at the Chatuchak Market.*
Above *These birds will be despatched for you at the market, or you can do the deed yourself at home.*

while the paste is being made. My recipes for curry pastes must be used just as a guide. They are not written in stone, it is not gospel and it is not rocket science. Sometimes, for instance, you may find that the shallots or the galangal you are using are sharper than usual, so touch, taste, smell and adjust. Needless to say, making a curry paste by hand is time-consuming, onerous and messy, but the result is genuinely superior – both in texture and balance of flavours – to one made in a food processor. Pastes made by hand have an integrity and intensity of flavour and the loving serenity that no machine can ever equal. However, these days, when everyone seems to lead such busy lives, you'll probably want to use the food processor.

One of the most agreeable things in fine Thai restaurants is the sight of serene but smiling ladies in traditional costume sitting cross-legged on a bench-cum-table carving fruit and vegetables into exquisite shapes to garnish so many Thai dishes. They spend years acquiring their exquisite art and it is a joy to watch their patient skill. If you have the time and the patience, you may wish to emulate them.

The Thai table and quantities

Eating Thai food (which, by the way, is not served as a procession of starter, vegetable, main course and pudding) is meant to be a sociable affair where all the dishes are presented as they are cooked. Soups come in a large bowl and are eaten throughout the meal, not before it, and, certainly in Thailand, the food is not necessarily served hot. Some food is placed on platters, passed around and eaten with a spoon and fork, not with chopsticks.

For some mad reason, food editors seem to require measurements, weights and cooking times all in precise detail. Now, most food in Thailand, and indeed throughout Asia, is cooked outside on the simplest of equipment by people who have never read a cookery book or watched a TV cookery programme, they just cook instinctively. If you have only a small amount of chicken, then you have only a small amount of chicken, so you stretch the meal with rice or noodles. Please be warned that all the measurements, cooking times and weights in this book are absolutely approximate. No Thai person would ever dream of weighing out 275 g/10 oz of noodles or 225 g/8 oz of rice.

Anyway, that is my lecture over. I hope it has been helpful!

Below *Preparing the ingredients for a curry at the famous Pet-Palo-Huahaheng Duck Restaurant.*
Opposite *These ladies were happy for me to try their food.*

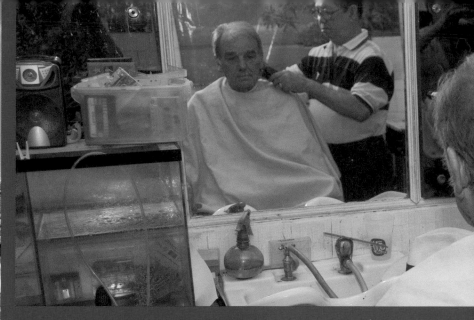

Sauces, pastes and dips

Above left to right *White onions. Fresh root ginger. Pet-Palo-Huahaheng Duck Restaurant.*

Sauces, pastes and dips

The Thai people like their food hot and some of the world's hottest chilli peppers are grown in Thailand. So, as you would expect, chillies play an important part in their curry sauces, pastes and dipping sauces.

These sauces and pastes are an indispensable part of Thai cooking, and home-made ones are well worth the effort. Many of the pastes can also be used as marinades, dipping sauces or to flavour a simply cooked bowl of rice or noodles. Chilli sauces are also used in salads.

Regional varieties are found throughout Thailand, but the basic curry pastes combine dry spices and fresh herbs with ginger, garlic, chillies and citrus juice and leaves.

Dipping sauces provide a contrast to the food they're served with – cooling dips for hot and spicy dishes, or fiery dips to accompany less highly flavoured food.

Below *Khun Phol Tantasathien, owner of the Spring Restaurant, was great company.*

41

Curry powder

1 tablespoon cloves

3 tablespoons coriander seeds

3 tablespoons cumin seeds

1 tablespoon fennel seeds

3 tablespoons dried chilli flakes

3 tablespoons turmeric powder

2 tablespoons ground ginger

2 teaspoons white peppercorns

4 cardamom pods

1 Heat a wok or heavy-based frying pan and, without adding any oil, dry-roast the cloves, coriander, cumin and fennel seeds for 40–50 seconds until they release their fragrance, then grind to a powder in a spice grinder.

2 Add the remaining ingredients to the ground spices in the grinder and whiz to a powder. Store in an airtight jar.

Below *Appreciating the shade at the Damnoen-Saduak floating market.*
Opposite *Dry-frying my spices for a curry paste, in the kitchens of the Intercontinental Hotel.*

The sauces and pastes below are used in recipes throughout the book. The dips, starting on page 51, will all go with kebabs, prawns and finger foods.

Thai green curry paste

1 teaspoon cumin seeds

1 teaspoon coriander seeds

6 fresh green chillies, chopped

a handful of finely chopped fresh basil leaves

1 tablespoon chopped fresh lemon grass

1 tablespoon chopped fresh coriander root or coriander leaves and stalks

2 red shallots, peeled and chopped

4 garlic cloves, peeled and chopped

1 cm / ½ inch piece galangal (Thai ginger) or fresh root ginger, peeled and finely chopped

4 or 5 kaffir lime leaves, finely chopped, or zest of 1 lime

6 black peppercorns

1 teaspoon shrimp paste

½ teaspoon salt

1 Heat a wok or heavy-based frying pan and, without adding any oil, dry-roast the cumin and coriander seeds for 40–50 seconds until they are toasted and aromatic. Tip into a spice grinder and grind to a powder.

2 Put the powder in a food processor with all the other ingredients and whiz to a fine paste (add a little water if the mixture is too stiff). Store in a jar in the fridge for 3–5 days.

Thai red curry paste

7 long, dried red chillies, deseeded

1 teaspoon cumin seeds

1½ teaspoons coriander seeds

¼ nutmeg, ground

2 tablespoons finely sliced fresh lemon grass

2 tablespoons finely chopped red shallots

1 tablespoon finely chopped roasted red shallots

1 tablespoon finely chopped garlic

zest of 2 limes, finely chopped

10 white peppercorns

a large pinch of salt

½ teaspoon shrimp paste

5 cloves

1 Soak the chillies in hot water for about 15 minutes, then drain.

2 Heat a wok or heavy-based frying pan and, without adding any oil, dry-roast the cumin and coriander seeds and the nutmeg for 40–50 seconds until they release their aroma. Tip into a spice grinder and grind to a powder.

3 Put the powder in a food processor with all the other ingredients and whiz to a paste (add a little water if the mixture is too stiff). Store in a jar in the fridge for 3–5 days.

Opposite Ingredients for the Thai red curry paste.

Thai yellow curry paste

1 teaspoon cumin seeds

2 teaspoons coriander seeds

6 fresh red chillies, chopped

½ teaspoon ground cinnamon

½ teaspoon ground cloves

1 fresh lemon grass stalk, chopped

2 red shallots, peeled and finely chopped

4 garlic cloves, peeled and finely
    chopped

2 tablespoons turmeric powder

1 teaspoon shrimp paste

½ teaspoon salt

1 Heat a wok or heavy-based frying pan and, without adding any oil, dry-roast the cumin and coriander seeds for 40–50 seconds until they are toasted and aromatic. Tip into a spice grinder and grind to a powder.

2 Put the powder in a food processor with all the other ingredients and whiz to a fine paste (add a little water if the mixture is too stiff). Store in a jar in the fridge for 3–5 days.

Thai massaman curry paste

This comes from southern Thailand.

3–4 dried red chillies

1 teaspoon cumin seeds

1 tablespoon coriander seeds

½ cinnamon stick, crushed

2–3 cloves

6 cardamom pods, crushed

5 black peppercorns

2 red shallots, peeled and finely chopped

1 fresh lemon grass stalk, finely chopped

3–4 garlic cloves, peeled and finely
    chopped

1 cm / ½ inch piece galangal (Thai
    ginger) or fresh root ginger, peeled
    and finely chopped

1 teaspoon shrimp paste

½ teaspoon salt

1 Soak the chillies in hot water for about 15 minutes, then drain.

2 Heat a wok or heavy-based frying pan and, without adding any oil, dry-roast the cumin and coriander seeds, cinnamon, cloves, cardamom pods and peppercorns for 40–50 seconds. Tip into a spice grinder and grind to a powder.

3 Put the powder in a food processor with all the other ingredients, including the chillies, and whiz to a fine paste (add a little water if the mixture is too stiff). Store in a jar in the fridge for 3–5 days.

Hanglay curry paste

This comes from northern Thailand.

1 tablespoon coriander seeds

1 tablespoon cumin seeds

5 dried red chillies, crushed

2 fresh lemon grass stalks, finely chopped

4 red shallots, peeled and finely chopped

2.5 cm / 1 inch piece fresh root ginger, peeled and finely chopped

2 tablespoons Demerara or palm sugar

1 tablespoon dark soy sauce

1 tablespoon shrimp paste

1 teaspoon turmeric powder

2 tablespoons Thai fish sauce (nam pla)

1 tablespoon tamarind pulp mixed with a little water (remember to remove the stones)

1 Heat a wok or heavy-based frying pan and, without adding any oil, dry-roast the coriander and cumin seeds for 40–50 seconds until toasted and aromatic. Tip into a spice grinder and grind to a powder.

2 Put the powder in a food processor with all the other ingredients and whiz to a fine paste (add a little water if the mixture is too stiff). Store in a jar in the fridge for 3–5 days.

Penang curry paste

This is one of many Malay influences to be found in Thailand.

1 teaspoon coriander seeds

15 dried red chillies, deseeded

3–4 red shallots, peeled and finely chopped

5 garlic cloves, peeled and finely chopped

1 fresh lemon grass stalk, finely chopped

2 tablespoons finely chopped fresh coriander root or coriander leaves and stalks

2.5 cm / 1 inch piece galangal (Thai ginger), finely chopped

2 tablespoons unsalted roasted peanuts, chopped

1 tablespoon shrimp paste

1 Heat a wok or heavy-based frying pan and, without adding any oil, dry-roast the coriander seeds for 40–50 seconds until toasted and aromatic.

2 Put the coriander seeds in a food processor with all the other ingredients and whiz to a thick paste (add a little water if the mixture is too stiff). Store in a jar in the fridge for 3–5 days.

Chiang Mai curry paste

1 tablespoon coriander seeds

2 teaspoons cumin seeds

2 red shallots, peeled and finely chopped

5 cm / 2 inch piece fresh root ginger,
  peeled and grated

2 large, fresh red chillies, deseeded and
  finely chopped

1 fresh lemon grass stalk, finely chopped

2 garlic cloves, peeled and finely
  chopped

½ teaspoon ground cinnamon

1 teaspoon turmeric powder

1 teaspoon shrimp paste

½ teaspoon salt

1 Heat a wok or heavy-based frying pan and, without adding any oil, dry-roast the coriander and cumin seeds for 40–50 seconds until toasted and aromatic. Tip into a spice grinder and grind to a fine powder.

2 Put the spice powder in a food processor with all the other ingredients and whiz to a paste (add a little water if the mixture is too stiff). Store in a jar in the fridge for 3–5 days.

Panaeng curry paste

Another one from southern Thailand.

1 teaspoon cumin seeds

4 red shallots, peeled and finely chopped

2 fresh lemon grass stalks, finely
  chopped

2 long, fresh red chillies, deseeded and
  finely chopped

2.5 cm / 1 inch piece fresh root ginger,
  peeled and finely chopped

5 garlic cloves, peeled and finely
  chopped

3 tablespoons unsalted roasted peanuts,
  roughly chopped

a handful of fresh coriander leaves and
  stalks, chopped

1 teaspoon shrimp paste

1 Heat a wok or heavy-based frying pan and, without adding any oil, dry-roast the cumin seeds for 40–50 seconds until they release their fragrance.

2 Put the cumin seeds in a food processor with all the other ingredients and whiz to a paste (add a little water if the mixture is too stiff). Store in a jar in the fridge for 3–5 days.

Above *Roadside barbeque stall on the Suriwongse Road, Bangkok.*

Peanut (satay) sauce

400 ml can thick coconut milk
3 tablespoons Demerara or palm sugar
2 tablespoons Thai Red Curry Paste (see
    page 45)
225 g/8 oz ground unsalted roasted
    peanuts
1 tablespoon Thai fish sauce (nam pla)

1 Mix all the ingredients in a saucepan and simmer for
15 minutes, stirring all the time. Use immediately or store
in a fridge and reheat as required.

Tamarind juice

Tamarind juice is used quite extensively in Thai cooking.

1 Mix 1 tablespoon of dried tamarind pulp with
2 tablespoons warm water (this will soften the pulp), then
mash well and strain to remove any seeds and fibres.

Marinades and dipping sauces

The next four recipes can be used as marinades or dipping sauces.

Coriander paste

2 tablespoons coarsely chopped fresh coriander
　　leaves and stalks
2 tablespoons coarsely chopped garlic
juice of 1 lime
1 teaspoon black peppercorns

1 Place all the ingredients in a blender or spice grinder, add a little water and whiz to a paste.

Thai sweet chilli sauce

6 tablespoons rice vinegar
2 tablespoons Demerara or palm sugar
1 fresh red chilli, finely chopped
½ teaspoon sweet paprika powder
2 tablespoons plum sauce
1 tablespoon Thai fish sauce (nam pla)
juice of 1 lime
2 garlic cloves, peeled and finely minced
1 teaspoon tomato paste
3 tablespoons water
1 teaspoon cornflour, mixed with a little cold
　　water to the consistency of single cream

1 Put all the ingredients into a small pan and bring to the boil.

2 Once it has boiled, reduce the heat to a simmer and cook for 5 minutes. Cool before using or serving.

Opposite *Getting down to work with Khun Phol Tantasathien, owner of the Spring Restaurant.*

Hot tiger sauce

4 tablespoons uncooked long-grain rice
1 tablespoon crushed, dried red bird's eye
　　chillies
5 tablespoons tamarind juice (see page 49)
2 tablespoons Thai fish sauce (nam pla)
2 tablespoons Demerara or palm sugar

1 Heat a dry, heavy-based frying pan and toast the uncooked rice until it is golden brown. Put the rice in a spice grinder and grind to a fine powder, then set aside.

2 Put the chillies in a bowl, add 1 tablespoon of the rice powder and mix well.

3 Add the rest of the ingredients and the remaining rice powder and stir well until you have a relatively thick sauce.

Hot and sweet garlic sauce

3 tablespoons Demerara or palm sugar
6 tablespoons water
6 tablespoons white wine vinegar
6 garlic cloves, peeled and finely minced
1 teaspoon salt
1 tablespoon chilli sauce

1 Put the sugar, water, vinegar, garlic and salt in a heavy-based saucepan and bring to the boil. When the sugar and salt have dissolved, reduce the heat and simmer the mixture until it has slightly reduced and thickened.

2 Add the chilli sauce and leave to cool, then pour into a sterilized jar and leave for a couple of days before using.

Dipping sauces

Universal Thai dipping sauce

1 tablespoon shrimp paste
3 tablespoons Thai fish sauce (nam pla)
juice of 2 limes
2 tablespoons soy sauce
3–4 garlic cloves, peeled and minced
5–6 dried red and green bird's eye chillies, very finely chopped
1 tablespoon Demerara or palm sugar
vegetable or groundnut oil, for frying

1 Heat a little oil in a wok or heavy-based pan and add the shrimp paste. Fry lightly until the paste starts to give off its aroma.

2 Put the shrimp paste in a blender or food processor with all the other ingredients and whiz together.

3 Pour into a small bowl for dipping.

Green mango dip
This is excellent with fish and seafood and any fresh vegetables.

225 g/8 oz shredded green (unripe) mango
6–8 garlic cloves, peeled and finely minced
2 tablespoons shrimp paste
2 tablespoons Thai fish sauce (nam pla)
juice of 2 limes
1 tablespoon Demerara or palm sugar

1 Put the mango, garlic and shrimp paste in a mortar and gently pound with a pestle to combine, but not mash, them.

2 Add the rest of the ingredients and mix well.

Hot, sweet and sour fish dipping sauce
This is a very versatile sauce and can be used to spice up any dish.

4–5 garlic cloves, peeled and finely chopped
4 tablespoons Thai fish sauce (nam pla)
8–10 dried red bird's eye chillies, finely chopped
2 teaspoons Demerara or palm sugar
6 tablespoons warm water
juice of 4 limes

1 Stir all the ingredients together and serve in a small bowl for dipping.

Barbeque dipping sauce (nam jim kiga)

6 tablespoons finely sliced small, fresh green chillies
6 tablespoons finely sliced small, fresh red chillies
4 tablespoons finely sliced red shallots
8 garlic cloves, peeled and finely chopped
4 tablespoons finely chopped fresh coriander leaves and stalks
juice of 2 limes
1 tablespoon Thai fish sauce (nam pla)
groundnut oil, for frying

1 Heat a little oil in a wok or heavy-based pan and gently fry the chillies, shallots and garlic until they are just soft and slightly golden.

2 Put in a food processor with all the other ingredients and whiz to a purée.

3 Serve in a bowl as a dipping sauce.

Opposite A peaceful way to sell your wares along the colourful waterfront of the Chao Phraya River.

Above *Abbot Pa at work decorating Wat Duangsoon, near Karasin in northeastern Thailand.*

Tomato and chilli dip

2 large, fresh red chillies
6 garlic cloves, peeled
3 red shallots, peeled and chopped into quarters
2 large ripe tomatoes
2 tablespoons Thai fish sauce (nam pla)
1 tablespoon chopped fresh coriander leaves and
    stalks
juice of 1 lime

1 Heat a wok or heavy-based frying pan and, without adding any oil, dry-roast the whole chillies for about 5 minutes, turning occasionally.

2 Add the garlic and shallots and dry-fry for another 5 minutes. The chilli skins should be darkened. Set aside to cool.

3 In the same pan, add the tomatoes and dry-fry for about 5 minutes until the skins have darkened.

4 Chop the stems off the chillies and cut the tomatoes into quarters.

5 Put the chillies, tomatoes, garlic and shallots into a food processor and whiz until you have a chunky salsa.

6 Put the salsa in a bowl and stir in the fish sauce, chopped coriander and lime juice.

Above *A family gather for lunch at Easan in northwestern Thailand.*

Chillies in oil

5 tablespoons vegetable oil
8 garlic cloves, peeled and finely chopped
3 red shallots, peeled and finely chopped
4 large, dried red chillies
2 tablespoons white caster sugar
1 teaspoon salt

1 Heat the oil in a wok or frying pan and fry the garlic until just turning brown, then remove and put to one side.

2 Do the same with the shallots.

3 Fry the chillies for a couple of minutes, then remove from the pan and, using a pestle and mortar, pound together with the shallots and garlic to a paste.

4 Reheat the oil (just to warm), add the pounded paste, sugar and salt and mix well. Pour into a serving dish.

Chilli jam
Makes one serving, multiply as necessary

75 ml / 3 fl oz vegetable oil
2 red shallots, peeled and finely chopped
2 garlic cloves, peeled and finely chopped
40 g / 1½ oz dried chilli flakes
½ teaspoon Demerara or palm sugar
salt, to taste

1 Heat the oil in a small saucepan and gently fry the shallots and garlic until just turning golden.

2 Add the chilli flakes and sugar and stir until well mixed.

3 Taste the sauce and season with salt as required.

Thai ginger dipping sauce

5 cm / 2 inch piece fresh root ginger, peeled and
    finely chopped
4 garlic cloves, peeled and finely chopped
2 tablespoons brown bean paste
1 fresh green chilli, finely chopped
2 tablespoons white wine vinegar
1 tablespoon soy sauce
1 tablespoon Demerara or palm sugar
2 tablespoons finely chopped fresh coriander
    leaves and stalks

1 Combine all the ingredients thoroughly and
serve immediately as a dipping sauce.

Plum sauce

250 ml / 8½ fl oz white wine vinegar
225 g / 8 oz white caster sugar
4 preserved plums (available in jars)

1 Put the vinegar and sugar in a saucepan and
bring to the boil, stirring. Once boiling, reduce
the heat and simmer for 15–20 minutes to make
a thick syrup.

2 Add the preserved plums and mash well,
then cook for another 2 minutes, stirring to form
a sauce.

Hot Thai salsa

½ cucumber, peeled, deseeded and chopped
    into fine cubes
4 spring onions, trimmed and finely chopped
8 radishes, finely chopped
5 cm / 2 inch piece fresh root ginger, peeled and
    grated
3 garlic cloves, peeled and minced
juice of 3 limes
a small handful of fresh mint, finely chopped
2 tablespoons white caster sugar
2 teaspoons chilli oil
salt, to taste

1 Combine all the ingredients in a large bowl and
season with salt.

2 Cover and leave in the fridge for about 1 hour
before serving to allow the juices to come out and
the flavours to develop.

Cucumber and pineapple relish

4 tablespoons rice vinegar
125 g / 4½ oz Demerara or palm sugar
1 cucumber, deseeded (leave on skin) and finely
    diced
½ pineapple, peeled, eyes and core removed,
    finely diced
75 g / 3 oz unsalted roasted peanuts, finely
    chopped
1 small, fresh red chilli, deseeded and finely
    chopped
1 teaspoon Thai fish sauce (nam pla)

1 Put the vinegar and sugar in a small saucepan
and bring to the boil. Reduce the heat and
simmer for about 5 minutes until the sugar is
fully dissolved.

2 Pour into a bowl and leave to cool.

3 Add all the other ingredients and mix well.

Left *Hot Thai salsa*

Rice dishes

Above left to right *The heat from the burners in these kitchens is intense. Fried rice in pineapple (see page 66). Grilled banana leaf parcels of sticky rice.*

Rice dishes

Have you taken rice?

Rice is the staple dish of Thailand. It does not accompany other dishes. Meat, fish or vegetables are seen as condiments to flavour the rice.

There is no particular word or phrase for 'food' in the Thai language and the question 'Have you eaten?' would be translated as 'Have you taken rice?'

Rice is served throughout the meal so it is a good investment to buy an electric rice cooker, which will, once the rice is cooked, keep it warm for ages without overcooking it. Long-grained jasmine rice is fragrant and the best. Sticky rice can be white or purply black grains. Black rice makes a great dessert.

I know an elderly Thai lady, called Miss Anna, who has eaten nothing but rice all her life. She has never eaten fish, meat or vegetables. At 86, she is hail and hearty and still enjoys 20 fags a day with her endless cups of green tea. She soaks her sticky, or glutinous, rice for about 5 hours and then strains and dries the rice before mixing in some coconut milk, a little sugar and a pinch of salt. She then stuffs the rice in a 30 or 38 cm/12 or 15 inch length of hollowed-out bamboo cane about one-third full and cooks it gently over a fire of dried coconut husks.

Below left to right *Farmer Sombat tending his rice at his farm at Na Karasin.*

Some essentials

Steamed rice

400 g / 14 oz jasmine rice

1 Rinse the rice until the water is clear (several times if necessary).

2 Put the rice in a saucepan with enough water to cover by about 2.5 cm / 1 inch, or put the rice in an electric rice cooker and add water according to the instructions.

3 Cover and cook gently for 10–12 minutes, then turn off the heat and leave to finish cooking for another 5–8 minutes.

Sticky rice

400 g / 14 oz sticky (glutinous) rice

1 Put the rice in a bowl, cover generously with cold water and leave overnight.

2 Line a bamboo steamer with muslin. Drain the rice and place it evenly in the steamer.

3 Place the steamer over a pan of simmering water, cover and steam for about 20 minutes until the rice is plump and tender.

4 Turn out into a large serving dish and fork it over to allow a certain amount of the excess steam to disperse.

Below *This young lady selling sticky rice in bamboo is obviously happy with her job.*

Sticky coconut rice

200 g / 7 oz sticky (glutinous) rice
175 ml / 6 fl oz coconut milk
1 tablespoon Demerara or palm sugar
1 heaped teaspoon salt

1 Prepare the sticky rice as on page 62 and place in a bowl.

2 Heat the coconut milk with the sugar and salt until the sugar has dissolved, then pour the coconut milk mixture over the rice and stir well.

3 Leave to stand for 10 minutes, then serve.

Right *Sticky (glutinous) rice.*

And, here are some personal favourites.

Fried rice with crab or prawns

2 red shallots, peeled and finely sliced
1 garlic clove, peeled and finely chopped
1 egg
250 g / 9 oz cooked rice
250 g / 9 oz steamed crab meat or
    cooked prawns (shelled and deveined)
1 fresh red chilli, deseeded and finely
    sliced
1 tablespoon light soy sauce
½ teaspoon Demerara or palm sugar
freshly ground black pepper, to taste
vegetable oil, for frying

To garnish
2 spring onions, trimmed and finely
    chopped
a handful of fresh coriander leaves,
    chopped

1 Heat a little oil in a wok or heavy-based frying pan. Add the shallots and stir-fry until slightly golden, then add the garlic. Continue stir-frying until the garlic has started to turn golden.

2 Break the egg into a bowl and beat until the yolk and white are well mixed. Pour into the wok and stir-fry until the egg has set.

3 Pour in the rice and stir-fry to mix well, then cook until starting to brown.

4 Stir in the crab or prawns and the chilli and mix in well with the rice. Then stir in the soy sauce, sugar and black pepper, to season.

5 Tip onto a serving dish and garnish with the chopped spring onions and coriander.

Fried rice with Chinese or Thai leaves

2 or 3 stalks of Chinese kale or pak choi
a handful of Chinese dried black
    mushrooms, soaked in warm water for
    about 20 minutes
1 garlic clove, peeled and finely chopped
8 large, raw tiger prawns, shelled and
    deveined (see page 145)
1 teaspoon Demerara or palm sugar
1 tablespoon soy sauce
1 tablespoon oyster sauce
250 g/9 oz cooked rice
vegetable oil, for frying

1 Remove any woody pieces of stalk from your chosen greens and slice the greens into pieces about 1 cm/ 1⁄2 inch long. Drain the mushrooms and discard the stems, then slice.

2 Heat some oil in a wok or heavy-based frying pan and fry the garlic until just becoming golden.

3 Add the mushrooms and stir-fry until they soften.

4 Add the greens and a little water and continue to stir-fry until the vegetables soften.

5 Add the prawns and stir-fry until they turn pink, then season with the sugar, soy and oyster sauces and mix well.

6 Add the rice and continue to stir-fry until the rice is hot and well mixed with the other ingredients. Transfer to a serving dish and serve.

Fried rice with prawns and bamboo shoots

a handful of Chinese dried black
    mushrooms, soaked in warm water for
    about 20 minutes
1 large, fresh red chilli, deseeded and
    finely chopped
225 g can bamboo shoots
8 large, raw tiger prawns, shelled and
    deveined (see page 145)
250 g/9 oz cooked rice
1⁄2 teaspoon Demerara or palm sugar
1⁄2 tablespoon light soy sauce
1⁄2 tablespoon oyster sauce
vegetable oil, for frying

To garnish
a handful of fresh coriander leaves,
    chopped
2 spring onions, trimmed and cut into
    2.5 cm/1 inch pieces

1 Drain the mushrooms and discard the stems, then slice.

2 Heat some oil in a wok or heavy-based frying pan and stir-fry the mushrooms, chilli and bamboo shoots for a couple of minutes.

3 Add the prawns and stir-fry until they turn pink.

4 Add the rice and stir-fry until the rice is beginning to colour and is well mixed with the other ingredients.

5 Season with the sugar, soy and oyster sauces and mix well.

6 Turn out onto a serving dish and garnish with the chopped coriander and spring onions.

Fried rice with roast pork

200 g/7 oz pork (fillet or similar)
1 teaspoon light soy sauce
½ teaspoon Demerara or palm sugar
½ tablespoon oyster sauce
2 garlic cloves, peeled and finely
    chopped
1 spring onion, trimmed and cut into
    2.5 cm/1 inch pieces
½ red onion, peeled and finely sliced
1 egg, beaten
250 g/9 oz cooked rice
½ tablespoon Thai fish sauce (nam pla)
vegetable oil, for frying

To garnish
¼ cucumber, deseeded and cut into
    small cubes
1 lemon, cut into small wedges, or a
    couple of limes, cut into quarters

1 Rub the pork with the soy sauce, sugar and half the oyster sauce and leave to marinate for about 1 hour.

2 Preheat the oven to 230°C/450°F/gas mark 8. Roast the pork for about 30 minutes until cooked and golden brown. Set aside to rest for about 10 minutes, then cut into bite-sized pieces.

3 Heat some oil in a wok or heavy-based frying pan and stir-fry the garlic, spring onion and red onion until soft and just turning brown.

4 Tip in the beaten egg and stir-fry until the egg is set.

5 Add the rice and roasted pork and continue to stir-fry until the rice is heated through and everything is mixed well.

6 Add the remaining oyster sauce and the fish sauce and stir well.

7 Tip the rice onto a serving dish, sprinkle with the diced cucumber, place the lemon or lime wedges around the dish and serve.

Below *Paddy fields at Na Karasin.*

Fried rice in pineapple

1 large fresh pineapple (leave on the
   leaves and stem)
2 tablespoons unsalted butter
$\frac{1}{2}$ red onion, peeled and cut into fine
   slices
2 slices cooked ham, cut into strips
a handful of cooked peas
a handful of sultanas
500 g / 1 lb 2 oz cooked rice
$\frac{1}{2}$ tablespoon light soy sauce
$\frac{1}{2}$ tablespoon oyster sauce
freshly ground black pepper, to taste
1 spring onion, trimmed and chopped,
   to garnish

1 Lay the pineapple on its side and cut lengthways down through the centre of the stem and leaves. Cut out the flesh, leaving each shell half intact. Cut the flesh into bite-sized cubes.

2 Melt the butter in a wok or heavy-based frying pan. Add the red onion and ham and stir-fry for about 30 seconds.

3 Add the pineapple, peas and sultanas and stir-fry for another 30 seconds, then add the rice and stir-fry to heat it through and mix well with the other ingredients. Season with the soy sauce, oyster sauce and black pepper.

4 Carefully spoon the fried rice mixture into the pineapple shells and garnish with the chopped spring onion.

Pan-fried rice with basil and coriander

3.5 cm / $1\frac{1}{2}$ inch piece pork fat, finely
   chopped
4 garlic cloves, peeled and finely chopped
3.5 cm / $1\frac{1}{2}$ inch piece fresh root ginger,
   peeled and grated
1 large, fresh red chilli, deseeded and
   finely chopped
2 skinless chicken thigh fillets, diced
100 g / $3\frac{1}{2}$ oz loin of pork, diced
500 g / 1 lb 2 oz cooked rice
2 teaspoons Golden Mountain sauce
   (a thin, salty, soybean sauce available
   from Asian shops), or Maggi seasoning
1 tablespoon Thai fish sauce (nam pla)
2 spring onions, trimmed and finely
   chopped
a handful of fresh coriander leaves,
   chopped
a handful of fresh basil, chopped
vegetable oil, for frying

1 Heat some oil in a wok or heavy-based frying pan. When the oil is hot, add the pork fat, garlic, ginger and chilli and stir-fry for a couple of minutes.

2 Add the diced chicken and pork and stir-fry for 3–4 minutes, or until the meat is golden and cooked through.

3 Add the rice and stir-fry, making sure all the ingredients are well mixed and the rice has heated through.

4 Season with the Golden Mountain or Maggi and fish sauces and stir in the chopped spring onions and herbs.

5 Tip out onto a serving dish and serve hot.

Oodles of noodles!

Above left to right *Thin and thick noodles. Cellophane noodles. Rice vermicelli.*

Oodles of noodles!

The vital ingredient

I love noodles so much, I could not live without them – spicy Asian noodle soups, deep-fried noodles, noodles with vegetables and chillies, noodles with oyster sauce, or indeed, their Mediterranean counterpart (some spaghetti, fettucini or tagliatelle, maybe just cooked al dente, tossed in olive oil with fresh basil leaves and shaved mature Parmesan cheese) will do me on any desert island. But, to untangle the mysteries and delights of Asian noodles and their European counterparts would take you years of research. Just have a (quick?) look at Alan Davidson's masterpiece *The Oxford Companion to Food*, which took him 20 years to create, and you will understand.

So, in brief, in the Thai kitchen noodles are a vital ingredient, as indeed they are throughout Asia (although not so much in India). They come in many shapes and sizes, are made from different ingredients and can be bought fresh or dried.

The Thais love all kinds of noodles, but they particularly like wide, flat noodles made from rice flour and known as rice stick noodles. Then you have the wheatflour and egg noodles known as hokkien noodles. They come in a variety of thicknesses and take only a short time to cook.

Cellophane noodles, which are very fine, dried, transparent noodles made from ground mung beans, only need plunging into hot water to soften before you use them. They go well cold with salads and, of course, hot in soups.

Rice vermicelli comes in various thicknesses and widths and needs only to be soaked in hot water and drained before use. It is also terribly good for deep-frying to make it crispy.

Unless I've specified otherwise, all noodles are the dried variety.

Crispy rice noodles (1)

75 g/3 oz rice vermicelli noodles, soaked
  in cold water for 20 minutes, then
  drained and dried
200 g/7 oz firm tofu, cut into thin strips
3 red shallots, peeled and finely sliced
3 garlic cloves, peeled and finely sliced
150 g/5 oz raw tiger prawns, shelled and
  deveined (see page 145)
juice of 1 lime
2 tablespoons plum sauce
1 tablespoon sweet chilli sauce
2 tablespoons Thai fish sauce (nam pla)
3 tablespoons Demerara or palm sugar
vegetable oil, for frying

To garnish

1 large, fresh red chilli, deseeded and
  finely sliced
3 spring onions, trimmed and finely
  chopped

1 Heat enough oil to deep-fry (7–10 cm/3–4 inches) in a
wok or heavy-based frying pan to a medium heat. Add
the noodles a handful at a time and when they puff up
(it takes seconds) turn them over to cook the other side.
When they have browned, lift them out and drain well on
kitchen paper. Repeat the process until all the noodles
are cooked.

2 Using the same pan, fry the tofu strips until they are crisp
and golden, then remove and drain on kitchen paper.

3 Do the same for the shallots and garlic and then the
prawns (cook until they have turned pink and are slightly
crispy).

4 Pour off most of the oil from the wok and return it to
the heat. Add the lime juice, plum sauce, sweet chilli
sauce, fish sauce and sugar and stir for about 5 minutes
over a low heat until the sauce starts to thicken.

5 Add half the noodles and quickly toss them around,
then add the shallots, garlic, prawns and tofu.

6 Place on a serving dish, crumble over the remaining
noodles and garnish with the chilli and spring onions.

Below *Helping out in the Charm Thai restaurant,
Intercontinental Hotel.*

Crispy rice noodles (2)

100 g/3½ oz rice vermicelli noodles,
 soaked in cold water for 20 minutes,
 then drained and dried
150 g/5 oz minced pork
100 g/3½ oz raw tiger prawns, shelled,
 deveined (see page 145) and finely
 chopped
3.5 cm/1½ inch piece fresh root ginger,
 peeled and grated
2 garlic cloves, peeled and finely chopped
1 tablespoon rice vinegar
2 tablespoons Thai fish sauce (nam pla)
2 tablespoons chilli sauce
2 tablespoons soft brown sugar
1 large, fresh red chilli, deseeded and
 finely chopped
vegetable oil, for deep-frying
1 bunch of fresh coriander, chopped,
 to garnish

1 Heat enough oil to deep-fry (7–10 cm/3–4 inches) in a wok or heavy-based frying pan to a medium heat. Add the noodles a handful at a time and when they puff up (it takes seconds) turn them over to cook the other side. When they have browned, lift them out and drain well on kitchen paper. Repeat the process until all the noodles are cooked.

2 Pour off most of the oil from the wok and return to the heat. Add the pork, prawns, ginger and garlic and stir-fry for a couple of minutes, or until the pork is golden brown.

3 Add the vinegar, fish sauce, chilli sauce, sugar and chopped chilli and stir until everything is boiling and well mixed.

4 Turn off the heat, add the fried noodles, stir quickly and serve immediately garnished with the chopped coriander.

Above *A colourful array of plates and noodle bowls of all sizes at Chatuchak Market.*

Crispy fried noodles

1 red onion, peeled and finely chopped

3 garlic cloves, peeled and finely chopped

2 teaspoons yellow bean sauce

2 tablespoons tomato paste

½ teaspoon white caster sugar

60 ml/2½ fl oz Thai fish sauce (nam pla)

60 ml/2½ fl oz tamarind juice (see page 49)

juice and zest of 1 lime

160 g/5½ oz fillet of pork, thinly sliced

450 g/1 lb thin rice vermicelli noodles, soaked in cold water for 5 minutes, then drained and dried

vegetable oil, for frying

2 spring onions, trimmed and chopped, to garnish

1 Heat some oil in a wok or heavy-based pan and stir-fry the onion, garlic, yellow bean sauce and tomato paste for 2–3 minutes.

2 Add the sugar, fish sauce and tamarind juice and bring to the boil, then stir in the lime juice and zest and the pork. Reduce the heat and cook, uncovered, for about 20 minutes, stirring occasionally.

3 Heat some oil in another wok or frying pan until smoking slightly. Throw in the noodles, a handful at a time. Fry on one side until golden, turn over and cook on the other side, then remove and drain on kitchen paper. Continue this process until all the noodles are cooked.

4 Put the noodles on a serving dish, pour over the pork mixture and garnish with the chopped spring onions.

Stir-fried glass noodles

100 g / 3½ oz glass noodles, soaked in
    cold water for 20 minutes, then
    drained
3 tablespoons dried wood ear
    mushrooms, soaked in warm water for
    30 minutes
3 garlic cloves, peeled and finely
    chopped
250 g / 9 oz thinly sliced raw chicken
1 carrot, peeled and shredded
1 stringed celery stick, shredded
    and cut into 5 cm / 2 inch lengths
60 ml / 2½ fl oz chicken stock
2 eggs, beaten
1 tablespoon rice vinegar
3 tablespoons Thai fish sauce (nam pla)
½ teaspoon white caster sugar
½ teaspoon salt
½ teaspoon freshly ground black pepper
2 spring onions, trimmed and cut into
    2.5 cm / 1 inch lengths
vegetable oil, for frying

1 Cut the noodles into 5 cm / 2 inch lengths. Drain the mushrooms and cut off the stems.

2 Heat some oil in a wok or heavy-based pan and stir-fry the garlic until it is just turning golden.

3 Add the chicken and stir-fry for a couple of minutes until the meat is cooked and turning brown.

4 Add the mushrooms, carrot and celery and stir-fry until everything is well mixed. Stir in the noodles, then the stock and mix well.

5 Push the contents to the side of the wok to create a well in the middle (add a little more oil if necessary) and pour in the beaten eggs, stirring until the egg is set, then stir into the noodle mixture.

6 Stir in the vinegar, fish sauce, sugar, salt, black pepper and spring onions and tip onto a serving dish. Serve immediately.

Right *Noodle seller.*

Stir-fried thin and flat noodles with prawns or chicken

3 garlic cloves, peeled and finely
  chopped
300 g / 11 oz large, raw tiger prawns,
  shelled and deveined (see page 145),
  or 300 g / 11 oz skinless chicken
  breast fillets, thinly sliced
3 tablespoons tamarind paste
2 tablespoons Thai fish sauce (nam pla)
2 tablespoons Demerara or palm sugar
2 eggs, beaten
150 g / 5 oz thin flat rice noodles, soaked
  in hot water for about 4 minutes, then
  drained
75 g / 3 oz chives, chopped
a pinch of chilli powder
2 tablespoons dried shrimp powder
2 tablespoons unsalted roasted peanuts,
  chopped
185 g / 6½ oz beansprouts
3 spring onions, trimmed and cut into
  2.5 cm / 1 inch pieces
vegetable oil, for frying

To garnish
1 large, fresh red chilli, deseeded and
  finely shredded
a handful of fresh coriander leaves,
  chopped
lime slices

1 Heat some oil in a wok or heavy-based pan and stir-fry the garlic until just turning golden.

2 Add the prawns or chicken and stir-fry for a couple of minutes, or until they are cooked. Remove from the wok and put aside in a warm place.

3 In a small bowl, mix the tamarind paste with the fish sauce and sugar.

4 Add a little more oil to the wok and pour in the beaten eggs, stirring until the eggs are scrambled and set. Add the prawns or chicken and the noodles and chives and stir-fry for a few seconds to mix well.

5 Add the tamarind mixture, chilli powder, dried shrimp and half the peanuts and stir well to combine.

6 Add the beansprouts and spring onions and stir-fry until the noodles are fully cooked.

7 Turn out onto a serving dish and garnish with the remaining peanuts, the chilli, chopped coriander and lime slices.

Opposite *Stir-fried thin and flat noodles with prawns.* Right *Tiger prawns.*

Above *A traditional celebration by monks at the Lam Pao reservoir in Kalasin province, northeastern Thailand.*

Stir-fried thick noodles with pork

1 dessertspoon oyster sauce

1 dessertspoon yellow bean sauce

1 dessertspoon light soy sauce

1 teaspoon Demerara or palm sugar

1 tablespoon cornflour

450 g/1 lb cooked, thick, flat rice
noodles mixed with 2 teaspoons soy
sauce

4 garlic cloves, peeled and finely
chopped

250 g/9 oz fillet of pork, finely sliced

175 g/6 oz pak choi, cut into 2.5 cm/
1 inch chunks

vegetable oil, for frying

For the seasoning sauce

2 large, fresh red chillies, deseeded and
finely chopped

3 tablespoons Thai fish sauce (nam pla)

1 tablespoon chilli sauce

3 tablespoons white caster sugar

3 tablespoons rice vinegar

1 First, in a small bowl, mix all the ingredients for the seasoning sauce, stir well and set aside.

2 In a small bowl, mix the oyster, yellow bean and soy sauces with the sugar, cornflour and 2 tablespoons of water and set aside.

3 Heat some oil in a wok or heavy-based pan and stir-fry the noodles for about 5 minutes, or until they start to brown. Transfer to a warm serving dish.

4 Heat a little more oil in the wok or pan and stir-fry the garlic until it is starting to turn golden. Add the pork and continue to stir-fry until the pork is golden and cooked – 5–7 minutes.

5 Add the pak choi and stir-fry for another minute or two, then tip in the prepared oyster sauce mixture. Mix well and stir-fry for another minute or so.

6 Pour this over the noodles and serve with the seasoning sauce on the side.

Above *The staff at the Spring Restaurant seem a bit nervous to have me in their midst.*

Stir-fried egg noodles with vegetables

1 tablespoon light soy sauce

2 tablespoons oyster sauce

1 teaspoon Demerara or palm sugar

4 garlic cloves, peeled and finely sliced

250 g/9 oz mixed, fresh vegetables, such as broccoli florets, green beans, baby sweetcorn, etc., cut into bite-sized pieces

250 g/9 oz fresh egg noodles

50 g/2 oz beansprouts

1 medium, fresh red chilli, deseeded and finely shredded

3 spring onions, trimmed and chopped

vegetable oil, for frying

chopped fresh coriander leaves, to garnish

1 In a small bowl, mix the soy sauce with the oyster sauce and sugar and set aside.

2 Heat some oil in a wok or heavy-based pan and stir-fry the garlic until lightly golden. Add all the mixed vegetables and stir-fry briskly for about 1 minute.

3 Add the noodles and oyster sauce mixture, mix well and stir-fry for a couple of minutes.

4 Add the beansprouts, chilli and spring onions and stir-fry for another minute.

5 Tip onto a serving dish and garnish with chopped coriander.

Vegetable rice noodles

8 wood ear mushrooms, soaked in warm
    water for 30 minutes
100 g/3½ oz firm bean curd, diced
3 garlic cloves, peeled and chopped
5 cm/2 inch piece fresh root ginger,
    peeled and finely grated
5 cm/2 inch piece carrot, peeled and
    grated
100 g/3½ oz green beans, cut into
    2.5 cm/1 inch lengths
½ red pepper, deseeded and cut into fine
    strips
2 tablespoons Golden Mountain sauce
    (a thin, salty, soybean sauce available
    from Asian shops) or Maggi seasoning
2 teaspoons Demerara or palm sugar
250 g/9 oz rice vermicelli noodles,
    soaked in hot water for about
    4 minutes, then drained and dried
100 g/3½ oz beansprouts
¼ white cabbage, finely shredded
vegetable oil, for frying
Thai Sweet Chilli Sauce (see page 51),
    to serve

1 Drain the mushrooms and discard the stems, then slice. Heat some oil in a wok or heavy-based pan and fry the bean curd until golden, then drain on kitchen paper and put to one side.

2 Stir-fry the garlic, ginger and bean curd for about 1 minute.

3 Add the carrot, green beans, red pepper and mushrooms and stir-fry for another couple of minutes.

4 Add the Golden Mountain or Maggie seasoning and sugar and mix well, then cover the wok and steam for 1 minute.

5 Add the noodles, beansprouts and cabbage and mix well, then cover and steam for another minute.

6 Turn onto a serving plate and serve with chilli sauce on the side.

Opposite When I visited Wat Whoalompong in the Silom area, I enjoyed a different sort of air-conditioned transport.

Muslim-style noodles

2 red shallots, peeled and chopped
3 dried red chillies
250 ml/8½ fl oz coconut milk mixed with
    250 ml/8½ fl oz water
250 g/9 oz fresh, wide rice noodles
250 g/9 oz thinly sliced fillet of beef
450 g/1 lb broccoli, cut into bite-sized
    pieces
60 ml/2½ fl oz tamarind juice (see page 49)
2 tablespoons sweet soy sauce
4 tablespoons Thai fish sauce (nam pla)
2 tablespoons Demerara or palm sugar

1 Put the shallots and chillies in a spice grinder and grind to a paste.

2 Heat the coconut milk and water in a wok or heavy-based frying pan until it boils and the oil from the coconut milk starts to separate.

3 Add the shallot mixture and cook, stirring, for about 3 minutes.

4 Add all the remaining ingredients and mix well. Cook for about a minute or so or until the noodles and beef are cooked, then serve.

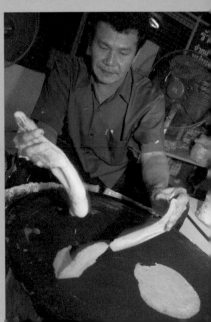

Salads, snacks and street food

Above left to right *If you get peckish along the Suriwongse Road, you can always try these fried locusts. Spicy crab with cucumber (see page 90). These stuffed calamari were very tasty.*

Salads, snacks and street food

... called desire

Street cooking in Thailand can range from spicy chicken

kebabs and satays to crushed, fiery green pawpaw salads, or

indeed just a slice of ripe mango sprinkled with chopped, dried

red chillies. It is unlikely that the purveyor or hawker, who may

be aged between 14 and 70 and who pushes his cart or tricycle

through the crowded, teeming streets, has ever read a cookbook or watched reality cooking TV shows or owns a set of scales. But, with the intuition born of taste, touch, smell and necessity, he can cook the pants off most of us.

Do you remember Martha and the Vandellas' great hit, covered by Mick Jagger and David Bowie, 'Dancing in the Street'? I think there should be a song that celebrates cooking in the street.

Below *This attractive young lady was selling coffee in the Chatuchak Market.*

Minced warm beef salad

2 tablespoons long-grain rice
450 g / 1 lb minced lean beef
juice of 1 lime
2 tablespoons Thai fish sauce (nam pla)
2.5 cm / 1 inch piece galangal (Thai
    ginger) or fresh root ginger, peeled
    and finely sliced
6 shallots, peeled and very finely sliced
4 spring onions, trimmed and chopped
2 fresh red chillies, finely chopped
    (deseeded if preferred)
2 tablespoons chopped fresh coriander
    leaves and stalks
crunchy salad leaves of your choice
a good handful of fresh mint leaves,
    to garnish

1 Heat a heavy-based pan and dry-fry the rice until brown, then grind to a powder in a spice grinder or food processor.

2 Mix the minced beef with the lime juice, fish sauce, galangal or ginger and the shallots.

3 Using a heavy-based saucepan on a medium heat, gently dry-fry the mixture in two batches for 8–10 minutes each batch, stirring with a spatula until the beef has broken up and is cooked.

4 Tip the beef mixture into a bowl and add the ground rice powder, spring onions, chillies and chopped coriander. Mix well.

5 Rip up the salad leaves, place on a serving dish to serve as a 'bowl', spoon in the beef salad and garnish with the mint leaves. Alternatively, spoon the beef salad into individual leaves.

Above *Preparing for a festival at Wat Duangsoon, near Karasin in northeastern Thailand.*

Beef salad with aubergine

150 g / 5 oz beef fillet, finely sliced no
    thicker than 5 mm / ¼ inch
a large pinch of salt
juice of 2 limes
a pinch of sugar
3 dried bird's eye chillies, crushed
4 red shallots, peeled and finely sliced
1 aubergine, topped and tailed and cut
    into bite-sized pieces
1 fresh lemon grass stalk, finely sliced
1 teaspoon chilli paste
2 tablespoons Thai fish sauce (nam pla)
3 kaffir lime leaves, finely shredded, or
    ½ tablespoon lime zest
vegetable oil, for frying

To garnish
1 large, fresh red chilli, deseeded and
    finely shredded
a handful of mixed fresh coriander and
    mint leaves

1 Put the beef in a bowl with the salt, lime juice and sugar and stir in the bird's eye chillies. Mix thoroughly and leave to one side for at least 15 minutes to allow the marinade to 'cook' the beef.

2 Heat some oil in a wok or heavy-based frying pan and add the shallots. Stir-fry for a couple of minutes, then add the aubergine chunks, lemon grass, chilli paste, fish sauce and lime leaves or zest. Stir-fry for about another 8 minutes, or until the aubergines are cooked.

3 Mix the beef and marinade with the aubergines and the cooking juices and garnish with the shredded chilli and the mint and coriander leaves.

Warm sour steak salad

350 g / 12 oz piece lean steak
2 tablespoons Thai fish sauce (nam pla)
juice of 3 limes
½ teaspoon roasted chilli powder
1 teaspoon Demerara or palm sugar
4 red shallots, peeled and finely sliced
salt and freshly ground black pepper
crunchy mixed salad leaves, to serve
a handful of mixed fresh mint and
    coriander leaves, chopped, to garnish

1 Season both sides of the steak with salt and black pepper.

2 Line a grill pan with foil and cook the beef under a preheated grill for 6–7 minutes on each side. When cooked, slice the beef into strips across the grain.

3 In a large bowl, mix the fish sauce with the lime juice, chilli powder and sugar and toss the beef and shallots in the dressing.

4 Serve the beef salad on a bed of salad leaves and garnish with the chopped mint and coriander.

Grilled hot and sour fish salad

2 mackerel or trout, gutted, cleaned and
    fins removed
2 fresh lemon grass stalks, finely sliced
3 red shallots, peeled and finely sliced
2 spring onions, trimmed and finely
    sliced
2.5 cm / 1 inch piece fresh root ginger,
    peeled and cut into fine strips
6 kaffir lime leaves, finely shredded, or
    1 tablespoon lime zest
juice of 3 limes
1 tablespoon Thai fish sauce (nam pla)
4 bird's eye chillies, finely sliced

To garnish
1 large, fresh red chilli, deseeded and
    finely sliced
a handful of fresh mint leaves, chopped

1 Place the fish under a preheated medium-hot grill and cook for about 10 minutes on each side. Once cooked, put aside to cool.

2 When the fish has cooled enough to handle, remove the skin and the bones and gently flake the flesh into bite-sized pieces.

3 In a bowl, mix the lemon grass with the shallots, spring onions, ginger, lime leaves or zest, the lime juice, fish sauce and bird's eye chillies. Add the fish to this mixture and gently fold together.

4 Tip onto a serving dish and garnish with the sliced red chilli and chopped mint.

Spicy crab with cucumber

225 g / 8 oz white crab meat, cooked and flaked

3 spring onions, peeled and chopped

1 fresh lemon grass stalk, bruised and finely sliced into rings

1 fresh red chilli, deseeded and finely chopped

juice of 2 limes

1 onion, peeled and finely chopped

2 hardboiled eggs, peeled and chopped

2 tablespoons Thai fish sauce (nam pla)

2 tablespoons chopped fresh coriander leaves and stalks

2 tablespoons Demerara or palm sugar

1 cucumber, peeled, deseeded and cut into 1 cm / ½ inch chunks

2 tablespoons rice vinegar

1 teaspoon salt

1 tablespoon water

1 In a large bowl, mix all the ingredients except 1 tablespoon of sugar and the cucumber, vinegar, salt and water. Cover and leave in the fridge for about 1 hour.

2 Put the cucumber in another bowl. Mix the sugar, vinegar, salt and water and pour over the cucumber. Leave to marinate for about 30 minutes, then drain off all the liquid.

3 Serve the crab salad in the centre of a serving dish surrounded by the cucumber.

Thai squid salad

450 g / 1 lb squid, cleaned
juice of 2 limes
3 garlic cloves, peeled and finely
    chopped
2 teaspoons chilli paste
1 tablespoon Demerara or palm sugar
3 tablespoons Thai fish sauce (nam pla)
1 red onion, peeled and cut into fine
    rings
175 g / 6 oz unsalted roasted peanuts,
    roughly chopped
salad leaves, to garnish

1 Cut open each squid tube lengthways to form a flat sheet and score the inside of the squid in a criss-cross pattern, then cut into bite-sized pieces.

2 Bring some water to the boil, add a little of the lime juice and blanch the squid for a minute or so, then remove, drain and set aside.

3 Put the garlic, chilli paste, remaining lime juice, the sugar and fish sauce in a bowl and mix well to make a dressing.

4 Mix the onion and peanuts with the blanched squid and pour over the dressing. Serve with a salad garnish.

Prawn and pink grapefruit salad

300 g / 11 oz large, raw tiger prawns,
    shelled and deveined (see page 145)
2 pink grapefruit
1 tablespoon Thai fish sauce (nam pla)
juice of 1 lime
1 tablespoon Chilli Jam (see page 55)
½ teaspoon white caster sugar
3 tablespoons fresh grated coconut,
    lightly toasted
3 red shallots, peeled and finely sliced
3 dried bird's eye chillies, crushed
10 fresh mint leaves
a handful of fresh coriander leaves

1 Boil some water in a large saucepan, add the prawns and boil for about 2 minutes, until the prawns are pink and cooked. Drain and set aside to cool.

2 Meanwhile, using a serrated knife, peel the skin off the grapefruit and cut out the segments between the pith.

3 In a small bowl, mix the fish sauce with the lime juice, chilli jam and sugar to make a dressing.

4 In a large bowl, combine the grapefruit, prawns, coconut, shallots, chillies, mint and coriander leaves. Pour over the dressing, mix well and serve.

Prawn and fruit salad

3 shallots, peeled and finely sliced

5 garlic cloves, peeled and very finely sliced

150 g/5 oz small, cooked prawns

½ green pawpaw, peeled, deseeded and cut into small cubes

1 large, ripe green apple, peeled, cored and chopped into small pieces (sprinkle with lemon juice to stop the apple going brown)

1 ripe pear, peeled, cored and cut into small pieces

½ pineapple, peeled, eyes and core removed, and cut into small chunks

100 g/3½ oz grapes, cut in half and deseeded

vegetable oil, for shallow-frying

a handful of fresh coriander leaves, chopped, to garnish

For the dressing

juice of 1 lime

zest of ½ lime

1 tablespoon Thai fish sauce (nam pla)

2 teaspoons Demerara sugar

1 medium, fresh red chilli, deseeded and finely chopped

1 Heat some oil in a wok or heavy-based frying pan and shallow-fry the shallots and garlic until they are crisp and golden. Using a slotted spoon, remove from the pan and drain on kitchen paper, then set aside.

2 Mix all the ingredients for the dressing in a large bowl.

3 Tip the prawns and all the fruit into the dressing and toss well, coating the ingredients.

4 Spoon onto a serving dish and sprinkle over the crispy garlic and shallots. Garnish with chopped coriander and serve.

Below *A boatman at the Damnoen-Saduak floating market. Just a two-hour drive from Bangkok, there are in fact three floating markets there: Ton Khem, Hia Kui and Khun Phithak.*

Chicken salad with papaya

250 ml / 8½ fl oz coconut cream
200 g / 7 oz skinless chicken breast fillets
2 garlic cloves, peeled and finely
    chopped
4 red shallots, peeled and finely sliced
3 small, fresh red chillies
2 tablespoons Thai fish sauce (nam pla)
1 teaspoon dried shrimp paste
10 cherry tomatoes, cut in half
150 g / 5 oz green papaya, peeled and
    grated
juice of 2 limes
a handful of fresh mint leaves, chopped
a handful of fresh coriander leaves,
    chopped

1 Pour the coconut cream into a pan and bring to the boil. Add the chicken breast, reduce the heat to a simmer and cook for about 5 minutes. Turn off the heat, cover the pan and leave the chicken breast in the cooling liquid for 20–25 minutes.

2 When the chicken has cooled, remove it from the pan and shred into small pieces.

3 Put the garlic, shallots and chillies in a food processor and whiz to a paste. Add the fish sauce and shrimp paste and whiz to combine.

4 Tip into a bowl, add the chicken, tomatoes, papaya, lime juice, mint and coriander leaves and combine well, then spoon onto a serving dish.

Chicken salad with fresh figs

2 cold, cooked, skinless chicken breasts,
    shredded
4–6 fresh figs, quartered
½ cucumber, peeled, deseeded and cut
    into 1 cm / ½ inch cubes
3 spring onions, trimmed and chopped
a good handful of fresh mint leaves,
    chopped
1 small iceberg lettuce, shredded
a good handful of unsalted roasted
    peanuts, chopped, to garnish

For the dressing
2–4 dried bird's eye chillies, crushed
2.5 cm / 1 inch piece galangal (Thai
    ginger) or fresh root ginger, peeled
    and grated
1 tablespoon soy sauce
1 tablespoon Thai fish sauce (nam pla)
juice of 3 limes
1 tablespoon honey

1 Combine all the ingredients for the dressing in a small bowl.

2 In another bowl, mix the chicken with the figs, cucumber, spring onions and chopped mint and pour over the dressing. Toss the mixture together lightly.

3 Arrange the iceberg lettuce on a serving dish and mound the salad on top. Garnish with the peanuts and serve.

Above *Birds awaiting the pot at Klong Toey Market. Bangkok's largest wet market, it caters for professional cooks rather than tourists.*

Minced duck salad

1 tablespoon long-grain rice
275 g/10 oz minced raw duck meat
juice of 2 limes
1 tablespoon Thai fish sauce (nam pla)
2 fresh lemon grass stalks, finely sliced
3 red shallots, peeled and finely sliced
5 spring onions, trimmed and finely
   chopped
4 kaffir lime leaves, finely sliced, or zest
   of 1 lime
½ teaspoon roasted chilli powder
a selection of crunchy salad leaves, to
   serve
a handful of fresh mint leaves, to garnish

1 Heat a heavy-based pan and dry-fry the rice until brown, then grind to a powder in a spice grinder or food processor.

2 Stir-fry the duck, lime juice and fish sauce in a wok or heavy-based frying pan until dry and browned. Tip into a bowl.

3 Add the ground rice powder, lemon grass, shallots, spring onions, lime leaves or zest and the chilli powder and combine well.

4 Serve on a bed of salad leaves and garnish with the mint leaves.

Green pawpaw salad

1 green pawpaw, peeled, deseeded and
    cut into 1 cm / ½ inch pieces
3 garlic cloves, peeled and finely chopped
2 teaspoons chilli paste
1 tablespoon Thai fish sauce (nam pla)
1 tablespoon Demerara or palm sugar
6 dried shrimps
juice of 1 lime
4 ripe tomatoes, skinned, deseeded and
    chopped
50 g / 2 oz fine green beans, blanched
    and cut into 2.5 cm / 1 inch pieces
3 tablespoons unsalted roasted peanuts,
    chopped
chopped fresh coriander or mint leaves,
    to garnish

1 Put 1 tablespoon of the pawpaw, the garlic, chilli paste, fish sauce, sugar, dried shrimps and lime juice in a food processor and whiz to a paste.

2 Put the rest of the pawpaw, the tomatoes, green beans and peanuts in a bowl and stir in the paste (if necessary add a little water to the paste to loosen it).

3 Serve garnished with the chopped herbs.

Left *I enjoyed preparing salads in the kitchens of the Charm Thai restaurant at the Intercontinental Hotel, Bangkok.*

Spicy carrot salad

4–6 carrots, peeled and grated
2–3 ripe plum tomatoes, skinned,
    deseeded and chopped
chopped fresh coriander and mint leaves,
    to garnish

For the dressing
2 bird's eye chillies or 1 large, fresh red
    chilli, deseeded and finely chopped
1 tablespoon unsalted roasted peanuts
juice of 2 limes
zest of 1 lime
1–2 garlic cloves, peeled and crushed
1 teaspoon dried shrimp powder or paste
1 tablespoon Thai fish sauce (nam pla)
1 teaspoon Demerara or palm sugar

1 Place all the ingredients for the dressing in a food processor and whiz to a fairly thick consistency. Pour into a bowl.

2 Add the carrots and tomatoes to the dressing and mix well, then leave in the fridge for at least 1 hour before serving. Garnish with the chopped herbs to serve.

Spicy pork salad

350 g / 12 oz minced pork
2 tablespoons unsalted roasted peanuts,
    finely chopped
1 red onion, peeled and finely chopped
4 spring onions, trimmed and chopped
1 large, fresh red chilli, finely chopped
3.5 cm / 1½ inch piece fresh root ginger,
    peeled and finely chopped
juice of 3 limes
zest of 1 lime
1 tablespoon Thai fish sauce (nam pla)
a good handful of fresh coriander leaves
    and stalks, finely chopped
crunchy lettuce leaves, to serve
salt, to taste

1 Dry-fry the pork in a heavy-based frying pan, stirring until the pork is half cooked.

2 Add the peanuts and continue to stir-fry until the pork is cooked. Drain off any cooking liquid and place the pork and peanuts in a bowl.

3 Mix in all the remaining ingredients except the lettuce, until thoroughly amalgamated.

4 Lay the lettuce leaves on a serving dish, pile the salad on top and serve.

Pork and prawn rice paper rolls

225 g / 8 oz pork shoulder, boiled in water
    for 30 minutes and left to cool
10–12 raw tiger prawns, shelled,
    deveined (see page 145) and boiled in
    water until just pink and curled
8 x 30 cm / 12 inch dried rice papers
1 small red-leafed lettuce or radicchio
    lettuce, leaves separated
115 g / 4 oz rice vermicelli noodles,
    cooked according to the instructions
    on the pack and cooled
a good handful of beansprouts
1 large, fresh red chilli, deseeded and
    cut into very fine strips, then cut into
    2.5 cm / 1 inch lengths
1 small bunch of fresh mint leaves

1 Carve the cooked pork into thin slices, about 2.5 x 6 cm / 1 x 2½ inches in length. Cut the cooked prawns in half.

2 Prepare a large bowl of warm water and spread out a clean, dry tea towel on a work surface.

3 Working with one sheet at a time, dip the dried rice papers into the water for about 10 seconds until each is soft. Remove from the bowl and gently lay flat on the tea towel to drain slightly.

4 Place a lettuce leaf (or half a leaf, depending on the size) onto the middle of each rice paper, then place a small amount of each of the other ingredients on the lettuce leaf.

5 Roll all these ingredients carefully together in the rice paper and trim the roll into small, neat cylinders, then place on a serving dish.

6 Repeat this process until you have used up all the ingredients and serve with a dipping sauce of your choice (see pages 51–57).

Above left to right *Walking through the Silom district of Bangkok, I came across these monks outside Wat Whoalompong. Monk Vichien was eager to talk and to practise his English.*

Chilli pork and pineapple bites

3 garlic cloves, peeled and finely
   chopped
225 g / 8 oz minced pork
1 spring onion, trimmed and finely sliced
½ tablespoon finely chopped fresh
   coriander leaves
25 g / 1 oz unsalted roasted peanuts,
   finely chopped
2 tablespoons light soy sauce
3 tablespoons Demerara or palm sugar
a pinch of freshly ground black pepper
16 pineapple chunks (fresh or canned)
1 large, fresh red chilli, deseeded and
   finely shredded
vegetable oil, for frying

1 Heat some oil in a wok or heavy-based frying pan and stir-fry the garlic until just turning golden.

2 Add the pork and stir-fry over a medium heat to break up any lumps and dry the mixture out.

3 Add the spring onion, chopped coriander, peanuts, soy sauce, sugar and black pepper and stir-fry for about 5 minutes until the mixture is sticky and dry. Remove from the heat.

4 Arrange the pineapple chunks on a serving dish and spoon a little of the pork mixture onto each chunk. Garnish with the shredded chilli and serve.

Thai soy bean fritters

1 large red onion, peeled and very finely
    chopped
2 large, fresh red chillies, deseeded and
    very finely chopped
1 cm / $\frac{1}{2}$ inch piece galangal (Thai ginger)
    or fresh root ginger, peeled and grated
zest of 1 lime
4 garlic cloves, peeled and very finely
    chopped
1 tablespoon Thai shrimp paste
225 g / 8 oz soy beans, cooked and
    puréed
2 eggs
2 tablespoons Thai fish sauce (nam pla)
2 tablespoons finely chopped fresh
    coriander leaves and stalks
1 dessertspoon cornflour
vegetable oil, for frying

1 Put the onion, chillies, galangal or ginger, the lime zest, garlic and shrimp paste in a food processor and whiz together until puréed.

2 Add the soy beans, eggs, fish sauce, chopped coriander and cornflour and mix well. Leave in the fridge for about 1 hour to firm up.

3 Pour some oil into a deep pan to a depth of at least 1 cm / $\frac{1}{2}$ inch and heat to about 180°C / 350°F.

4 Dip your hands in a little cold water and form the soy bean mixture into patties 3.5 cm / $1\frac{1}{2}$ inches in diameter.

5 Gently lower the patties into the hot oil 3 or 4 at a time – do not crowd the pan – and cook until golden brown. Remove with a slotted spoon, drain on kitchen paper and put aside to keep warm. Continue this process until all the patties are cooked.

6 Arrange the patties on a serving dish and serve with a dip of your choice (see pages 51–57).

Thai fish cakes

450 g / 1 lb firm, white fish fillets,
    skinned, boned and roughly chopped
1 tablespoon Thai Red Curry Paste (see
    page 45)
1 tablespoon Thai fish sauce (nam pla)
1 egg, beaten
50 g / 2 oz snake beans or French green
    beans, finely chopped
4 kaffir lime leaves, finely shredded, or
    zest of 1 lime
1 medium, fresh red chilli, deseeded and
    finely chopped
vegetable oil, for frying
Thai Sweet Chilli Sauce (see page 51),
    to serve

1 Put the fish in a food processor and whiz to a smooth paste. Add the curry paste, fish sauce and egg and blend into the fish.

2 Tip this mixture into a bowl and add the beans, lime leaves or zest and the chopped chilli. Dip your hands in a little cold water and shape the fish mixture into small patties about 5 cm / 2 inches across.

3 Heat about 5 cm / 2 inches of oil in a wok or heavy-based frying pan. Drop 1 teaspoon of the mixture into the oil – if it sizzles, the oil is ready for frying.

4 Fry the fish cakes in small batches on both sides until golden. Remove with a slotted spoon, drain on kitchen paper and set aside to keep warm while you fry the rest.

5 Serve with the chilli dipping sauce.

Gold purses

Makes 30

115 g/4 oz raw, shelled and deveined
   prawns (see page 145), minced
75 g/3 oz canned water chestnuts,
   drained and chopped
1 spring onion, trimmed and finely
   chopped
1 garlic clove, peeled and finely chopped
1 tablespoon oyster sauce
30 wonton sheets, cut into 7 cm/3 inch
   squares
salt and freshly ground black pepper, to
   taste
vegetable oil, for deep-frying
Thai Sweet Chilli Sauce (see page 51),
   to serve

1 In a small bowl, mix the prawns with the water chestnuts, spring onion, garlic and oyster sauce and season with salt and black pepper.

2 Place about $\frac{1}{2}$ teaspoon of this mixture onto the middle of each wonton square. Moisten the edges of the wonton square and, using your finger, bring up the edges and squeeze together to form a little purse. Continue until you have used up all the mixture.

3 Heat about 5 cm/2 inches of oil until sizzling but not too hot. Carefully lower 4 or 5 of the purses into the oil and cook for 3–4 minutes until golden brown. Remove with a slotted spoon, drain on kitchen paper and put aside to keep warm. Continue this process until all the purses are cooked.

4 Arrange the purses on a serving dish and serve with the chilli dipping sauce.

Spicy corn cakes

400 g/14 oz sweetcorn kernels (drained, canned sweetcorn is perfect)

3 red shallots, peeled and finely chopped

1 large, fresh red chilli, deseeded and finely chopped

1 egg, beaten

3 tablespoons rice flour

1 tablespoon Thai Yellow Curry Paste (see page 46)

a handful of fresh coriander leaves, chopped

1 tablespoon Thai fish sauce (nam pla)

vegetable oil, for shallow-frying

Cucumber and Pineapple Relish (see page 57), to serve

1 Thoroughly mix all the ingredients except the oil in a bowl, until you have a soft mixture.

2 Dip your hands in a little cold water and shape the mixture into small patties about 5 cm/2 inches across.

3 Heat about 5 cm/2 inches of oil in a wok or heavy-based frying pan and shallow-fry the patties in small batches until they are golden – about 2 minutes on each side. Remove with a slotted spoon, drain on kitchen paper and set aside to keep warm while you fry the rest.

4 Serve hot with the cucumber and pineapple relish.

Below *An array of Thai beers and other drinks at the Pet-Palo-Huahaheng Duck Restaurant.*

Skewered green prawns with coriander and chilli

350 g/12 oz raw tiger prawns, heads and
  shells removed, tails left on, and
  deveined (see page 145)
4 long bamboo skewers

For the marinade

1 garlic clove, peeled and finely chopped
1 large, fresh red chilli, deseeded and
  finely chopped
juice of ½ lime
2 teaspoons light soy sauce
1 tablespoon oyster sauce
1 tablespoon finely chopped fresh
  coriander leaves
1 teaspoon sesame oil
1 teaspoon vegetable oil

1 Mix all the ingredients for the marinade in a bowl.

2 Place the prawns in the marinade and mix well to coat, then cover and leave in the fridge overnight.

3 Soak the bamboo skewers in cold water for about 1 hour to stop them burning.

4 Remove the prawns from the marinade (keep the marinade) and thread them onto the bamboo skewers.

5 Line a grill pan with foil and cook the prawns under a preheated grill for about 8 minutes on each side, brushing occasionally with the marinade – do not place the prawns too near the grill as they will burn and dry out. Serve hot.

Sticky rice with prawns and freshly grated coconut

enough Sticky Rice (see page 62) cooked
  with Sticky Coconut Rice (see page
  63) to serve 4 people
2 garlic cloves, peeled and chopped
4 fresh coriander roots, chopped
a pinch of freshly ground black pepper
200 g/7 oz raw tiger prawns, shelled,
  deveined (see page 145) and minced
25 g/1 oz grated fresh coconut
1 teaspoon Thai fish sauce (nam pla)
3 tablespoons Demerara or palm sugar
vegetable oil, for frying
5 kaffir lime leaves, finely sliced, or zest
  of 1 lime, to garnish

For the coconut topping

150 g/5 oz grated fresh coconut
2 tablespoons water
50 g/2 oz Demerara or palm sugar

1 Prepare the rice.

2 Using a small blender or spice grinder, blend the garlic, coriander roots and black pepper to a paste.

3 Heat some oil in a wok or heavy-based frying pan and stir-fry this mixture for a minute or two until it gives off its fragrance.

4 Add the minced prawns, coconut, fish sauce and sugar and stir-fry for about 4 minutes. Tip out into a bowl and set aside.

5 To make the coconut topping, mix the coconut with the water and sugar in a pan and stir over a low heat until the sugar has just dissolved. Remove from the heat.

6 To serve, fill a small bowl with the sticky rice and turn it out onto a serving dish to make a neat mound. Top with the prawn mixture, then the coconut topping and garnish with the lime leaves or zest.

Pandanus leaves stuffed with chicken

You might have to search long and hard to find fresh pandanus leaves (which come from the screw pine), but if you can find them, this is a great little snack dish. However, you may be able to buy them frozen, in which case, defrost them carefully and dry them thoroughly before using.

600 g / 1 lb 5 oz skinless chicken breast
    fillets, cut into bite-sized cubes
20 pandanus leaves, cleaned and dried
vegetable oil, for deep-frying

For the marinade
4 garlic cloves, peeled and chopped
4 fresh coriander roots, chopped
a pinch of salt
1 teaspoon ground white pepper
2 tablespoons oyster sauce
1½ tablespoons sesame oil
1 tablespoon plain flour

1 Prepare the marinade. Using a small food processor or spice grinder, whiz the garlic, coriander roots, salt and white pepper to a paste.

2 Tip the paste into a bowl, add the oyster sauce, sesame oil and flour and mix well.

3 Add the chicken and mix thoroughly so that the chicken is well coated, then cover and leave in the fridge for at least 4–5 hours.

4 To make the pandanus leaf parcels, fold each pandanus leaf in half lengthways to make a cup. Place a piece of the chicken in this, wrap one of the long ends around the side and over the chicken, and tuck in the spare end to enclose the chicken. Repeat until all the chicken is wrapped.

5 Heat enough oil for deep-frying (at least 5 cm / 2 inches) in a large wok or heavy-based pan and deep-fry the parcels 3 or 4 at a time for 8–10 minutes, or until they feel firm to the touch. Using a slotted spoon, remove from the pan, drain on kitchen paper and keep them warm while you cook the remainder.

6 Arrange the parcels on a serving dish and serve hot with plum sauce. (Note: you unwrap the chicken from the leaf to eat – the leaves are discarded.)

Above *Rush-hour traffic in the Chidlom area of Bangkok, where you can shop till you drop.*

Curried pasties

1 packet frozen puff pastry, defrosted,
    rolled quite thinly and cut into
    7.5 cm / 3 inch discs
vegetable oil, for deep-frying

For the filling

2 tablespoons vegetable oil
1 small red onion, peeled and finely
    diced
200 g / 7 oz minced, raw chicken
1 small red pepper, deseeded and finely
    diced
50 g / 2 oz cooked peas
3 garlic cloves, peeled and finely
    chopped
2 tablespoons Demerara or palm sugar
350 g / 12 oz peeled, cooked potatoes,
    cut into very small cubes
3 tablespoons Thai fish sauce (nam pla)
1 teaspoon Thai curry powder
a handful of fresh coriander leaves, finely
    chopped

1 To make the filling, heat the oil in a wok or heavy-based frying pan and stir-fry the onion for a couple of minutes until softened and slightly brown.

2 Add the chicken and stir-fry until all the lumps have separated and the chicken is cooked.

3 Add the diced pepper, peas, garlic and sugar and stir-fry for a couple of minutes, then stir in the potatoes, fish sauce, curry powder and chopped coriander and cook for 2–3 minutes. Remove from the pan and place in a bowl.

4 Take a disc of the pastry and put 1 tablespoon of the chicken mixture in the middle. Brush the edges of the pastry with water, then pull up the sides and crimp the edges together tightly to form a pasty. Repeat with the remaining discs until you have used up all the filling.

5 Heat enough oil for deep-frying (at least 5 cm / 2 inches) in a large wok or heavy-based pan and deep-fry the pasties 3 or 4 at a time until they are puffed and golden. Using a slotted spoon, remove from the pan, drain on kitchen paper and keep them warm while you cook the remainder. Serve hot or cold.

Above *This barbecue stall in the Suriwongse Road was just the place for a late-night snack.*
Opposite top to bottom *At the end of a hard day, what better than a cocktail or two with my friends at the Intercontinental Hotel. I don't think I was supposed to cook my own skewers, but it was good fun.*

Satay chicken

1 kg / 2¼ lb skinless chicken breast fillets,
    cut into 3.5 x 10 cm / 1½ x 4 inch strips
40 bamboo skewers
Satay Sauce (see page 49), to serve

For the marinade
3 red shallots, peeled and chopped
4 garlic cloves, peeled and chopped
4 fresh coriander roots, chopped
2.5 cm / 1 inch piece fresh root ginger,
    peeled and chopped
1 tablespoon coriander seeds
1 tablespoon cumin seeds
1 tablespoon turmeric powder
1 teaspoon curry powder
2 tablespoons light soy sauce
400 ml / 14 fl oz coconut milk
4 tablespoons vegetable oil
2 tablespoons Demerara or palm sugar
1 teaspoon salt

1 To make the marinade, put the shallots, garlic, coriander roots and ginger in a food processor, whiz to a paste and tip into a bowl.

2 Dry-fry the coriander seeds, cumin seeds and turmeric until giving off their aroma, then grind to a powder in a spice grinder. Add the ground spices to the garlic paste along with the curry powder, soy sauce, coconut milk, oil, sugar and salt and mix well.

3 Add the chicken to the marinade, mixing well to make sure that all the chicken is well coated, then cover and leave to marinate in the fridge for at least 6 hours, turning every so often.

4 Soak the bamboo skewers in cold water for about 1 hour to stop them burning. Thread the chicken strips onto the skewers lengthways and cook under a preheated grill for 10 minutes on each side or until the chicken is cooked and slightly blackened. Serve hot with satay sauce.

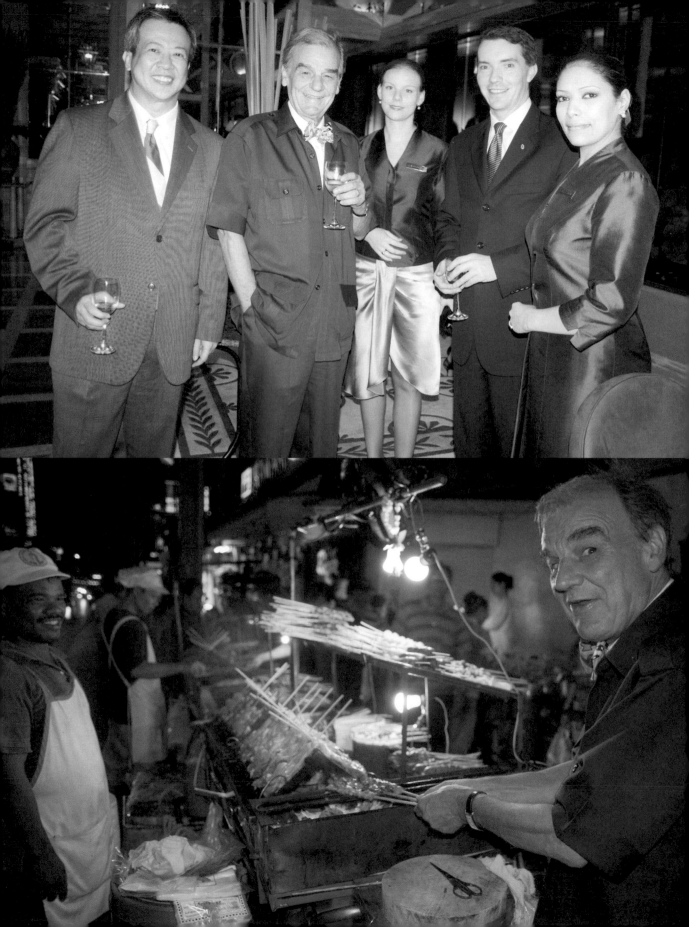

Soups

Above left to right *Spring onions. Chicken and vegetable clear soup (see page 115). Mr Hota was a charming host in his little tearoom.*

Soups
The Thai feel-good factor

In Western food culture, soup is presented in many menus under that horrible title of 'starters'. Throughout time, big bowls of soup were served with a louche, which is, of course, French for 'ladle', but is transposed into quasi-English intellectual argot as 'someone who is a little louche is a profligate, irresponsible hedonist', like me.

Soup for those of the poorer classes, such as my maternal grandmother, might have meant dried pea green soup simmered with a pork or a ham bone. In the early morning markets of France it might have been a simple beef stock and onion soup, maybe with some melted cheese and croutons. On a Cornish or an Italian fishing boat it might have been fish, simmered in a fish kettle, which years later, of course, was refined into the French bouillabaisse. So you have a cross of cultures. Hearty soups created to feed people of limited resources, and finely honed compositions to grace the 'starters' on the European and Western menus.

But soups are an essential part of the Thai table and, in the Thai way of life, they are not served as a beginning, an entrée or a starter, but placed upon the laden table alongside the rest of the meal. They might be hot and sour, clear soups, infused with tamarind, lemon grass, lime leaves, lime juice and fish sauce that explode on your palate, and might include prawns, chicken or simple fresh green vegetables; or they might be clear light soups, such as pork and vermicelli; or creamy, coconut milk concoctions like chicken, ginger or galangal soup and the chowder-like rib-sticking crab and sweetcorn soup. However, I repeat, they are not served as 'starters', but presented along with the other dishes, presented as a Thai feast. Here are some of my favourites.

Thai pumpkin soup

350 g / 12 oz peeled pumpkin, cut into
  chunks
1 litre/ 1¾ pints vegetable stock
150 ml / 5 fl oz mango juice or puréed
  canned mango and syrup
2 tablespoons peanut butter
3 spring onions, trimmed and finely
  chopped
2 tablespoons rice vinegar
1 cm / ½ inch piece fresh root ginger,
  peeled and grated
3 dried bird's eye chillies, crushed
1 garlic clove, peeled and minced
1 teaspoon grated orange zest
chopped fresh coriander leaves, to garnish

1 Place the pumpkin, stock and mango juice in a saucepan and bring to the boil. Reduce the heat and simmer, uncovered, for about 15 minutes, or until the pumpkin is soft.

2 When the pumpkin mixture is ready, pour into a food processor with the peanut butter and whiz until the mixture is smooth.

3 Return to the pan and add all the remaining ingredients except the coriander, then heat for about 5 minutes.

4 Pour into individual bowls, garnish with the chopped coriander and serve.

Hot and sour mushroom soup

1 litre/ 1¾ pints vegetable stock
225 g / 8 oz oyster mushrooms or other
  fungi of your choice
5 cm / 2 inch piece fresh lemon grass
  stalk, chopped into very fine rings
2 fresh red chillies, finely chopped
4 kaffir lime leaves, torn into pieces, or
  zest of 1 lime
juice of 2 limes
1 teaspoon Demerara or palm sugar
chopped fresh coriander leaves, to garnish

1 Pour the stock into a large pan and bring to the boil.

2 Add all the remaining ingredients except the coriander, reduce the heat and simmer, uncovered, until the mushrooms are just cooked.

3 Serve garnished with the chopped coriander.

Chicken, ginger and mushroom soup

750 ml / 1¼ pints coconut milk
5 cm / 2 inch piece fresh root ginger,
    peeled and sliced
2 fresh lemon grass stalks, crushed
4 red shallots, peeled and cut into
    quarters
400 g / 14 oz skinless chicken breast
    fillets, cut into slices
1 tablespoon Demerara or palm sugar
2 tablespoons Thai fish sauce (nam pla)
150 g / 5 oz straw mushrooms
200 g / 7 oz cherry tomatoes
juice of 2 limes
6 kaffir lime leaves, chopped, or
    1 tablespoon lime zest
2 large, fresh red chillies, deseeded and
    finely sliced
fresh coriander leaves, to garnish

1 Put the coconut milk, ginger, lemon grass and shallots in a large saucepan and bring to the boil. Reduce the heat to a simmer, add the chicken, sugar and fish sauce and cook for 5 minutes or so, or until the chicken is cooked through.

2 Add the mushrooms and tomatoes and cook for a further 3–4 minutes.

3 Add the lime juice, lime leaves or zest and the chillies just before serving and serve garnished with coriander leaves.

Chicken and coconut milk soup

400 ml can coconut milk
450 ml / 15 fl oz chicken stock
2 skinless chicken breast fillets, cut into
    bite-sized pieces
115 g / 4 oz oyster mushrooms
2 fresh lemon grass stalks, cut into fine
    rings
zest and juice of 1 lime
3 fresh green chillies, finely chopped
2.5 cm / 1 inch piece fresh root ginger,
    peeled and finely chopped
1 tablespoon Thai fish sauce (nam pla)
2 tablespoons chopped fresh coriander
    leaves and stalks, plus extra chopped
    leaves, to garnish

1 Pour the coconut milk and stock into a large pan and heat until the oil starts to come out of the coconut milk.

2 Add all the remaining ingredients, except the coriander for garnish, and simmer, uncovered, for 8–10 minutes.

3 Serve garnished with chopped coriander.

Chicken and vegetable clear soup

1 litre/1¾ pints chicken or vegetable
   stock
1 fresh red chilli, deseeded and finely
   chopped
1 fresh lemon grass stalk, cut into
   2.5 cm/1 inch pieces and crushed
juice and zest of 1 lime
2 skinless chicken breast fillets, cut into
   bite-sized pieces
1 carrot, peeled and cut into 5 cm/
   2 inch pieces
115 g/4 oz fine green beans, cut into
   2.5 cm/1 inch pieces
115 g/4 oz mangetout, cut into
   2.5 cm/1 inch pieces
3 spring onions, trimmed and chopped
   (use the green as well as the white
   part)
2 tablespoons chopped fresh coriander
   leaves and stalks
4 radishes, finely sliced
1 tablespoon Thai fish sauce (nam pla)

1 Put the stock, chilli, lemon grass and lime juice and zest in a large saucepan and bring to the boil. Reduce the heat and simmer, uncovered, for about 15 minutes, then add the chicken and cook for a further 5–7 minutes.

2 Meanwhile, using a vegetable peeler, shave the carrot pieces into fine strips. Add to the pan with all the remaining ingredients and cook for a further 2–3 minutes. Serve hot.

Duck and noodle soup

This soup requires a very specific, home-made stock.

For the stock

2 whole star anise

1 small cinnamon stick

1 whole duck, washed

2.5 litres / 4 pints water

10 garlic cloves, peeled and crushed

5 fresh coriander roots, crushed

2.5 cm / 1 inch piece fresh root ginger,
   peeled and roughly chopped

2 tablespoons Demerara or palm sugar

60 ml / 2½ fl oz Thai fish sauce (nam pla)

60 ml / 2½ fl oz dark soy sauce

1 teaspoon black peppercorns

1 dessertspoon salt

For the soup

1 kg / 2¼ lb fresh, wide rice noodles

2 tablespoons garlic-flavoured oil (see
   step 3, page 118)

450 g / 1 lb beansprouts, blanched for
   2 minutes

½ head lettuce leaves, roughly torn

To garnish

3 spring onions, trimmed and finely
   sliced

1 large, fresh red chilli, deseeded and
   finely sliced

fresh coriander leaves

freshly ground white pepper, to taste

For the chilli vinegar

3 fresh green chillies, finely sliced

cider vinegar

1 First make the stock. Dry-fry the star anise and cinnamon stick in a frying pan for 30–40 seconds until they release their fragrance.

2 Place them in a large pan or stockpot with all the other stock ingredients and bring to the boil. Reduce the heat to a simmer, cover the pan and simmer very gently until the duck is tender, but not falling apart – about 1½ hours.

3 Meanwhile, make the chilli vinegar. Put the sliced chillies in a small bowl and just cover with vinegar. Put to one side.

4 Remove the duck from the stock and allow to cool. Strain the stock of all the solid particles, return to the pan and keep warm over a low heat.

5 Pull all the meat off the duck, cut the meat into bite-sized pieces and set aside.

6 Heat the noodles in boiling water for about 1 minute until soft, then drain and place a portion each in the bottom of individual bowls.

7 To each bowl add 1 teaspoon garlic oil, some beansprouts, several pieces of lettuce leaf and 6–7 pieces of duck, then pour over stock to cover.

8 Garnish with the spring onions, sliced chilli, coriander leaves and white pepper and offer the chilli vinegar as an additional garnish.

Opposite top to bottom Preparing the stock for the duck and noodle soup at the Pet-Palo-Huahaheng Duck Restaurant. The finished soup.

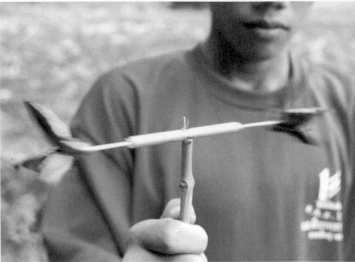

Above left to right *This malaeng thap beetle has luminous green wings. I was told this curious contraption was a beetle merry-go-round.*

Prawn, chicken and rice soup

1 fresh coriander root, finely chopped

4 garlic cloves, peeled and finely
  chopped

a pinch of freshly ground white pepper

75 g / 3 oz minced raw chicken

2 spring onions, trimmed and finely
  chopped

1 litre/ 1¾ pints chicken stock

2 tablespoons light soy sauce

2 teaspoons preserved or pickled radish
  slices

300 g / 11 oz cooked jasmine rice

100 g / 3½ oz raw tiger prawns, shelled
  and deveined (see page 145)

2.5 cm / 1 inch piece fresh root ginger,
  peeled and finely shredded

1 Chinese cabbage leaf (or use pak choi),
  roughly chopped

salt, to taste

vegetable oil, for frying

chopped fresh coriander leaves,
  to garnish

1 Using a spice grinder or small blender, whiz together the coriander root, 1 teaspoon of the chopped garlic, the white pepper and salt to form a paste.

2 Place the minced chicken, spring onions and coriander paste in a bowl and mix well, then shape into small balls, 1–1.5 cm / ½–¾ inch across.

3 Heat some oil in a wok or heavy-based frying pan and fry the remainder of the garlic until it is just turning brown. Scoop out the garlic and discard it (this is to flavour the oil). Put the oil to one side.

4 Pour the stock into a saucepan and bring to the boil, then add the soy sauce, radish slices and rice. Reduce the heat to a simmer.

5 Gently lower the meatballs into the stock and cook for 5 minutes, or until the chicken is cooked.

6 Add the prawns, ginger and Chinese cabbage or pak choi and cook for another couple of minutes, or until the prawns turn pink and butterfly.

7 Serve garnished with chopped coriander and the garlic oil drizzled over the top.

Prawn and lemon grass soup

3 medium, dried red chillies

2 red shallots, peeled

2 garlic cloves, peeled

10 raw tiger prawns, shelled and
  deveined (see page 145)

1.5 litres / 2½ pints chicken stock

3 fresh lemon grass stalks (use only the
  bottom of the stalk), thinly sliced

4 thin slices peeled fresh root ginger

3 kaffir lime leaves, chopped, or
  ½ tablespoon lime zest

1 fresh coriander root, chopped

4 tablespoons Thai fish sauce (nam pla)

2 tablespoons Tamarind Juice (see
  page 49)

2 teaspoons Demerara or palm sugar

chopped fresh coriander leaves,
  to garnish

1 Dry-fry the dried chillies in a wok or heavy-based frying pan over a low heat until dark and giving off their fragrance. Remove from the pan and, when cool, remove the stems and deseed them.

2 In the same pan, dry-fry the shallots and garlic over a low heat until soft and blistered. Remove from the pan and, when cool, slice finely. Set aside.

3 Dry-fry the prawns until they are pink and slightly coloured on both sides – 3–5 minutes, then set aside.

4 Pour the stock into a large pan and bring to the boil, then reduce the heat to a simmer. Add the roasted dried chillies, shallots and garlic, the lemon grass, ginger, lime leaves or zest and the coriander root and simmer for about 5 minutes, stirring constantly.

5 Add the prawns and stir in the fish sauce, tamarind juice and sugar.

6 Serve garnished with chopped coriander.

Below *Thai fish sauce (nam pla)*

Hot and sour prawn soup

This soup is probably one of the most well-known and loved dishes in Thailand.

350 g / 12 oz large, raw tiger prawns,
    shelled (reserve the heads and shells)
    and deveined (see page 145)
3 fresh lemon grass stalks: 1 stalk
    crushed, 2 stalks finely sliced
1 cm / ½ inch piece fresh root ginger,
    peeled and finely sliced
2 litres / 3½ pints chicken stock
6 bird's eye chillies, bruised
5 kaffir lime leaves, sliced, or zest of
    1 lime
2 spring onions, trimmed and finely
    sliced
2 tablespoons Thai fish sauce (nam pla)
75 g / 3 oz straw mushrooms
juice of 2 limes
vegetable oil, for frying
chopped fresh coriander leaves,
    to garnish

1 Heat some oil in a deep pan and fry the prawn heads and shells for about 5 minutes until they change colour.

2 Add the crushed lemon grass stalk together with the ginger and stock to the pan and bring to the boil, then reduce the heat and simmer, uncovered, for 20 minutes.

3 Strain the stock into another pan, discarding the prawn heads and shells, ginger and lemon grass.

4 Add the sliced lemon grass to the strained stock with the chillies, lime leaves or zest, the spring onions, fish sauce and mushrooms and cook over a medium heat for a couple of minutes.

5 Add the prawns and cook for 2–3 minutes, or until the prawns curl and turn pink.

6 Remove from the heat and add the lime juice. Serve garnished with chopped coriander.

Below *Eating in Thailand is a sociable affair.*

Prawn and pumpkin soup

2 red onions, peeled and chopped

1 medium, fresh red chilli, deseeded and
finely chopped

1 fresh lemon grass stalk, finely sliced

1 teaspoon shrimp paste

1 teaspoon Demerara or palm sugar

325 ml / 11 fl oz coconut milk

1 teaspoon tamarind paste

250 ml / 8½ fl oz water

500 g / 1 lb 2 oz pumpkin, peeled,
deseeded and cut into bite-sized
chunks

juice of 2 limes

8 raw tiger prawns, shelled and deveined
(see page 145)

100 ml / 3½ fl oz coconut cream

1 tablespoon Thai fish sauce (nam pla)

a handful of fresh basil leaves

1 Using a food processor, whiz together the onions, chilli, lemon grass, shrimp paste, sugar and about 2 tablespoons of the coconut milk to form a paste.

2 Put the paste in a large pan, add the rest of the coconut milk, the tamarind paste and water and stir until smooth.

3 Add the pumpkin and lime juice and bring the mixture to the boil, then reduce the heat and simmer, uncovered, for about 10 minutes, or until the pumpkin is tender.

4 Add the prawns and coconut cream and simmer for about 3 minutes, or until the prawns are curling and have turned pink.

5 Stir in the fish sauce and basil leaves and serve hot.

Crab and corn soup

6 garlic cloves, peeled and finely
chopped

6 red shallots, peeled and chopped

2 fresh lemon grass stalks, finely
chopped

3.5 cm / 1½ inch piece fresh root ginger,
peeled and grated

1 litre / 1¾ pints chicken stock

200 ml / 7 fl oz coconut milk

198 g can sweetcorn, drained

2 x 170 g cans crab meat

2 tablespoons Thai fish sauce (nam pla)

juice of 2 limes

1 teaspoon soft brown sugar

freshly ground black pepper, to taste

vegetable oil, for frying

chopped fresh coriander leaves,
to garnish

1 Heat some oil in a wok or heavy-based frying pan, add the garlic, shallots, lemon grass and ginger and stir-fry over a medium heat for 2 minutes until just turning colour.

2 Add the stock and coconut milk to the pan and bring to the boil. Add the sweetcorn and cook for 5 minutes.

3 Stir in the crab meat, fish sauce, lime juice and sugar and cook to heat through.

4 Season with black pepper, garnish with chopped coriander and serve.

Sweet and sour soup with sliced monkfish

1 teaspoon freshly ground black pepper

3 tablespoons chopped fresh coriander
    root

4 red shallots, peeled and finely chopped

1 teaspoon shrimp paste

1 fillet of monkfish, skinned and
    membrane removed, then cut into
    thin discs

2.5 cm / 1 inch piece fresh root ginger,
    peeled and finely chopped

1 litre/ 1¾ pints boiling water

3 teaspoons Demerara or palm sugar

1 dessertspoon Thai fish sauce (nam pla)

1 dessertspoon Tamarind Juice (see
    page 49)

juice of ½ lime

salt, to taste

vegetable oil, for frying

To garnish

1 large, fresh red chilli, deseeded and
    finely sliced

2 spring onions, trimmed and finely
    chopped

chopped fresh coriander leaves

1 Using a spice grinder or small blender, blend the black pepper, coriander root, shallots, shrimp paste and salt to taste to a paste.

2 Heat some vegetable oil in a pan and cook the paste until it releases its fragrance. Add the monkfish and ginger and stir-fry until just cooked.

3 Add the boiling water and season with the sugar, fish sauce, tamarind juice and lime juice.

4 Serve garnished with the sliced chilli and chopped spring onions and coriander.

Right *Just one of the vast complex of intricate buildings that make up the amazing Royal Grand Palace in Bangkok.*

Above *The charming staff of the aptly named Charm Thai restaurant at the Intercontinental Hotel, with my friend Marcel Nosari, executive chef, on the right.*

Pork and vermicelli soup

10–12 Chinese dried black mushrooms, soaked in warm water for 5–7 minutes

4 garlic cloves, peeled and finely chopped

450 g / 1 lb minced pork

a handful of chopped fresh coriander leaves, plus extra to garnish

650 ml / 1 pint 2 fl oz chicken stock

2 tablespoons light soy sauce

50 g / 2 oz glass vermicelli noodles, soaked in hot water for 5–6 minutes, drained and dried

salt and freshly ground black pepper, to taste

vegetable oil, for frying

1 Drain the mushrooms, discard the stems and cut into slices.

2 Stir-fry the garlic in a little oil in a wok or heavy-based frying pan until it is just turning golden. Using a slotted spoon, remove the garlic from the oil and drain on kitchen paper. Put the oil and garlic to one side.

3 In a small bowl, combine the pork with the chopped coriander, salt and black pepper. Wet your hands and shape into small balls about 1 cm / ½ inch across.

4 Pour the stock into a large pan and bring to the boil. Reduce the heat to a simmer, then add the soy sauce and place the pork balls in the stock. Simmer gently for 3 minutes, then add the mushrooms and noodles and cook for 2 minutes, stirring.

5 Serve sprinkled with the browned garlic, garlic oil and chopped coriander.

Vegetables

  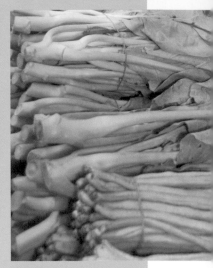

Above left to right *Beautifully fresh heads of broccoli. Tamarind paste. Chinese broccoli, grown in Thailand.*

Vegetables
Of snake beans, greens and more

In the frozen Fifties, on a Sunday morning in the bleak and dark November dawn, my father would tell me to gather the frosted, nutty Brussels sprouts from their ugly stalks. Then I lifted a root of horseradish from the icy loam for my mother to crush with vinegar and cream. The meat was in the stove and the fat was dripping gently over the parboiled and raked spuds, retrieved earlier from their store in the coal shed. The kitchen was steamy and smelling of food and life. The windows were

Above left to right *Sweetcorn. Stir-frying under the watchful eye of sous chef Salam Kaewjeerath. Crunchy, fresh beansprouts.*

dripping in condensation. There was some winter kale and some carrots, too. Simple fare for simple folk, and good.

But when you go to Thailand you will see, not the winter, but the sunshine on your plate. Cook on, eat on.

By the way, if you are on holiday and cooking in Thailand, you will buy very, very long, curled-up green beans, which are used in all kinds of dishes. They are called snake beans, but you can happily use French green beans, topped and tailed and cut into appropriate lengths, according to the recipe.

Green bean curry

1 tablespoon Thai Green Curry Paste (see
    page 45)
400 ml can coconut milk
600 ml / 1 pint chicken stock
450 g / 1 lb snake beans or French
    beans, cut into 5 cm / 2 inch pieces
250 g can bamboo shoots, drained
2 spring onions, trimmed and chopped
vegetable or coconut oil, for frying
2 tablespoons chopped fresh coriander,
    to garnish

1 Heat a little oil in a deep pan, add the curry paste and
stir-fry for a minute or two.

2 Add the coconut milk and cook until the oil from the
milk begins to separate.

3 Add the stock, beans, bamboo shoots and spring
onions and bring to the boil, then reduce the heat and
simmer gently for 15–20 minutes until the beans are
quite soft and the liquid is slightly reduced.

4 Garnish with chopped coriander and serve with plain,
boiled rice.

Stir-fried green beans and cauliflower

4 garlic cloves, peeled
a handful of fresh coriander leaves and
    stalks, chopped
2 tablespoons Thai fish sauce (nam pla)
1 teaspoon Demerara or palm sugar
$\frac{1}{2}$ teaspoon turmeric powder
a good handful of baby spinach leaves
$\frac{1}{2}$ teaspoon cracked black pepper
400 g / 14 oz cauliflower florets
120 ml / 4 fl oz water
200 g / 7 oz green beans, cut into 5 cm /
    2 inch lengths
5 spring onions, trimmed and cut into
    5 cm / 2 inch lengths
juice of 1 lime
vegetable oil, for frying

1 Crush 3 of the garlic cloves and finely slice the
remaining clove. Using a spice grinder or small blender,
blend the chopped coriander, crushed garlic,
1 tablespoon of the fish sauce, the sugar and turmeric
to make a paste.

2 Heat some oil in a wok or heavy-based frying pan and
stir-fry the sliced garlic for 30 seconds until just turning
golden, then remove from the pan and drain on kitchen
paper.

3 Using the same pan, stir-fry the spinach until just
wilted. Add the black pepper and remaining fish sauce
and mix well, then remove from the pan and keep warm
on a serving dish.

4 Using the same pan, heat a little more oil, add the
coriander paste and stir-fry for about 1 minute, until it
gives off its fragrance. Add the cauliflower and stir-fry for
a minute or so, then add the water, bring to a simmer,
cover the pan and cook for 3 minutes.

5 Add the beans, cover again and cook for 3 minutes, then
add the spring onions and stir-fry until they have wilted.

6 Spoon the vegetables over the spinach, sprinkle over
the lime juice and fried garlic and serve.

Above *Some of the stupas in the gardens of Wat Duangsoon. Stupas are dome-shaped monuments, used to house Buddhist relics.*

Aubergines with tofu

3 garlic cloves, peeled and finely
    chopped
3 or 4 aubergines (depending on size),
    topped and tailed, partly peeled and
    sliced
115 g/4 oz firm tofu, cut into 1 cm/
    ½ inch cubes
2 large, fresh red chillies, finely chopped
1 tablespoon yellow bean sauce
15 basil leaves
vegetable oil, for frying

1 Heat some oil in a heavy-based wok or frying pan and quickly fry the garlic until very light brown.

2 Add the aubergines and tofu and cook for another 5–7 minutes, turning to brown all sides.

3 Add all the remaining ingredients and mix gently to heat through. Serve immediately.

Above *A novice monk at Wat Duangsoon.*

Baby aubergines with cherry tomatoes

2 aubergines, topped and tailed and cut
 into bite-sized chunks
1½ tablespoons Thai fish sauce (nam
 pla)
2 red shallots, peeled and finely chopped
1 medium, fresh red chilli, deseeded and
 chopped
5 cm / 2 inch piece fresh root ginger,
 peeled and finely chopped
1 garlic clove, peeled and finely chopped
150 g / 5 oz cherry tomatoes
2 tablespoons malt vinegar
2 tablespoons Demerara or palm sugar
a handful of fresh basil leaves
vegetable oil, for frying

1 Place the aubergine chunks in a bowl and mix with
½ tablespoon of the fish sauce. Place the aubergines in a
bamboo steamer lined with greaseproof paper and steam
over boiling water for about 10 minutes.

2 Heat some oil in a wok or heavy-based frying pan and
stir-fry the shallots, chilli, ginger and garlic for about
30 seconds.

3 Add the steamed aubergine and the tomatoes and mix
well, then add the vinegar, the remaining fish sauce and
the sugar and stir-fry for about 3 minutes until the sauce
thickens.

4 Stir in the basil leaves and serve.

Stir-fried spinach

3 tomatoes, skinned, deseeded and cut
    into slices
2 large, fresh red chillies, chopped
4 garlic cloves, peeled and crushed
2 tablespoons soybean paste
900 g / 2 lb baby spinach leaves
freshly ground black pepper, to taste
vegetable oil, for frying

1 Heat some oil in a wok or heavy-based frying pan and stir-fry the tomatoes, chillies, garlic and soybean paste for a minute or so.

2 Add the spinach and season with black pepper, then stir-fry for another 2 minutes until just wilted, but do not overcook. Serve immediately.

Beansprouts with tomatoes

4 garlic cloves, peeled and finely chopped
2 tablespoons soybean paste
1 red onion, peeled and sliced
1 large, fresh red chilli, finely chopped
4 ripe tomatoes, deseeded and cut into
    quarters
2 spring onions, trimmed and chopped
4 double handfuls of beansprouts
vegetable oil, for frying
2 tablespoons freshly chopped coriander,
    to garnish

1 Heat some oil in a wok or heavy-based frying pan and stir-fry the garlic and soybean paste for about 1 minute.

2 Add the onion, chilli, tomatoes, spring onions and beansprouts and stir-fry for another couple of minutes.

3 Pour onto a serving dish, garnish with chopped coriander and serve.

Vegetable-stuffed omelette

3 tomatoes, skinned, deseeded and
    diced
I red onion, peeled and coarsely diced
100 g / 3½ oz courgettes, diced
2 spring onions, trimmed and chopped
1 fresh red chilli, deseeded and finely
    chopped
2 tablespoons finely chopped fresh
    coriander leaves
2 teaspoons Thai fish sauce (nam pla)
2 teaspoons soy sauce
1 teaspoon Demerara or palm sugar
6 eggs, beaten
vegetable oil, for frying

1 Heat some oil in a wok or heavy-based frying pan and stir-fry the tomatoes, onion, courgettes, spring onions, chilli and chopped coriander for 2–3 minutes.

2 Stir in the fish sauce, soy sauce and sugar and set this mixture aside.

3 Heat a little vegetable oil in another pan. Add one-quarter of the beaten eggs per person and make 4 omelettes.

4 Stuff the omelettes with the vegetable mixture and serve hot.

Pineapple curry

2 shallots, peeled and sliced
1 tablespoon Thai Red Curry Paste (see
    page 45)
1 fresh pineapple, peeled, eyes and core
    removed, and cut into 2.5 cm / 1 inch
    chunks
2 tablespoons Demerara or palm sugar
1 tablespoon Thai fish sauce (nam pla)
400 ml can coconut milk
300 ml / 10 fl oz vegetable or chicken
    stock
vegetable oil, for frying
chopped fresh coriander or mint leaves,
    to garnish

1 Heat some oil in a wok or heavy-based frying pan and gently fry the shallots for 1–2 minutes.

2 Add the curry paste and stir-fry for about 30 seconds, then add the pineapple and stir-fry for a few seconds until it is well mixed in.

3 Stir in the sugar and fish sauce, then add the coconut milk and stock and simmer for about 10 minutes.

4 Serve garnished with the chopped herbs.

Stir-fried vegetables (1)

3 fresh lemon grass stalks, white part
   only, finely chopped

4 garlic cloves, peeled and finely
   chopped

100 g / 3½ oz snake beans or French
   beans, cut into 5 cm / 2 inch pieces

2 stringed celery sticks, cut into 5 cm /
   2 inch pieces

1 large, fresh red chilli, deseeded and
   finely chopped

½ red pepper, deseeded and cut into thin
   5 cm / 2 inch pieces

1 bunch of asparagus, cut into 5 cm /
   2 inch pieces

1–2 tablespoons chilli sauce

2 tablespoons Thai fish sauce (nam pla)

1 teaspoon Golden Mountain sauce (a
   thin, salty, soybean sauce available
   from Asian shops), or Maggi
   seasoning

100 g / 3½ oz beansprouts

1 tablespoon unsalted roasted peanuts,
   chopped

a handful of fresh coriander leaves,
   chopped

vegetable oil, for frying

1 Heat some oil in a wok or heavy-based frying pan and stir-fry the lemon grass and garlic for a minute or so.

2 Add the beans, celery and chopped chilli and stir-fry for another minute or so.

3 Add the red pepper and asparagus and mix well, then cover and leave to steam for about 1 minute.

4 Add the chilli sauce, fish sauce and Golden Mountain or Maggi seasoning and mix well.

5 Add the beansprouts, mix everything together and serve sprinkled with the peanuts and chopped coriander.

Opposite *A joint effort as sous chef Salam and I get frying.*
Right *Garlands of beautiful Thai flowers to welcome your friends.*

Stir-fried vegetables (2)

50 g / 2 oz broccoli florets

50 g / 2 oz thin French beans, cut into
    5 cm / 2 inch lengths

5 baby sweetcorn

5 thin asparagus spears, cut into 5 cm /
    2 inch lengths

25 g / 1 oz mangetout, topped and tailed

100 g / 3½ oz mixed red and yellow
    peppers, deseeded and finely sliced

1 small carrot, peeled, cut into 5 cm /
    2 inch lengths and finely sliced

1 tablespoon Thai fish sauce (nam pla)

1 tablespoon oyster sauce

½ teaspoon white caster sugar

2 tablespoons water

4 garlic cloves, peeled and finely
    chopped

2.5 cm / 1 inch piece fresh root ginger,
    peeled and shredded

2 spring onions, trimmed and cut into
    5 cm / 2 inch lengths (both white and
    green parts)

salt

vegetable oil, for frying

1 Blanch the broccoli florets, beans and sweetcorn in boiling, salted water for 30 seconds, then remove and plunge into a bowl of iced water to stop them cooking further. Drain and mix with the asparagus, mangetout, sliced peppers and carrot.

2 In a small bowl, mix the fish and oyster sauces with the sugar and water.

3 Heat some oil in a wok or heavy-based frying pan and stir-fry the garlic and ginger until just turning golden.

4 Add the vegetables and stir-fry for about 30 seconds, then add the sauce mix, increase the heat and stir-fry for 3 minutes.

5 Just before serving, stir in the spring onions.

Right *The farmer's son checks out the sweetcorn at Sombat's farm near Na Karasin.*

Stir-fried asparagus

1 tablespoon pickled green peppercorns, rinsed and finely crushed

a handful of fresh coriander leaves, chopped

1 bunch of thin asparagus, cut into 5 cm / 2 inch lengths

a handful of French beans, cut into 5 cm / 2 inch lengths

2 garlic cloves, peeled and finely chopped

1 teaspoon Demerara or palm sugar

2 teaspoons water

1 tablespoon Thai fish sauce (nam pla)

1 large, fresh red chilli, deseeded and chopped

vegetable oil, for frying

1 In a small bowl, mix the crushed peppercorns with the chopped coriander.

2 Heat some oil in a wok or heavy-based frying pan and add the crushed pepper and coriander mixture, the asparagus, beans, garlic and sugar. Stir-fry for about 30 seconds to mix well, then add the water.

3 Cover the pan and steam for about 2 minutes, or until the vegetables are tender.

4 Season with the fish sauce and stir in the chopped chilli, then tip onto a serving dish and serve hot.

Green vegetable curry

2 tablespoons Thai Green Curry Paste (see page 45)

1 red onion, peeled, halved and cut into slices

400 ml can coconut milk

250 ml / 8½ fl oz water

300 g / 11 oz sweet potato, peeled and cut into bite-sized chunks

200 g / 7 oz aubergine, topped and tailed and cut into bite-sized chunks

150 g / 5 oz green beans, cut into 5 cm / 2 inch lengths

6 kaffir lime leaves, or 1 tablespoon lime zest

2 tablespoons Thai fish sauce (nam pla)

juice of 2 limes

zest of 1 lime

2 teaspoons Demerara or palm sugar

vegetable or coconut oil, for frying

a handful of fresh coriander leaves, chopped, to garnish

1 Heat some oil in a large wok or heavy-based frying pan and stir-fry the curry paste and onion for about 3 minutes.

2 Add the coconut milk and water and bring to the boil, then reduce the heat and simmer for about 5 minutes.

3 Add the sweet potato and cook for 5–6 minutes.

4 Add the aubergine, beans and lime leaves or zest and cook for 10 minutes, or until the vegetables are tender, stirring occasionally.

5 Add the fish sauce, lime juice and zest and sugar and mix well.

6 Serve sprinkled with the chopped coriander.

Above *Kaffir lime leaves, fresh and dried*

Red vegetable curry

2 tablespoons Thai Red Curry Paste (see page 45)

1 red onion, peeled, cut in half and sliced

400 ml can coconut milk

3 tablespoons water

350 g / 12 oz peeled potatoes, cut into bite-sized cubes

200 g / 7 oz cauliflower florets

6 kaffir lime leaves, or 1 tablespoon lime zest

150 g / 5 oz French beans, cut into 5 cm / 2 inch pieces

8 baby sweetcorn, cut in half lengthways

½ red pepper, deseeded and cut into thin strips

1 tablespoon chopped pickled green peppercorns

2 tablespoons Thai fish sauce (nam pla)

juice of 1 lime

2 teaspoons Demerara or palm sugar

a handful of fresh coriander leaves, chopped

vegetable or coconut oil, for frying

1 Heat some oil in a large wok or heavy-based frying pan and stir-fry the curry paste and onion for 4–5 minutes.

2 Add the coconut milk and water and bring to the boil, then reduce the heat and simmer for 5 minutes.

3 Add the potatoes, cauliflower and lime leaves or zest and simmer for 6 minutes.

4 Add the beans, sweetcorn, red pepper and peppercorns and cook for a further 5 minutes, or until the vegetables are tender.

5 Add the fish sauce, lime juice, sugar and chopped coriander, stir well and serve with steamed rice.

Above *This charming young lady was selling Chinese broccoli, a member of the mustard family. It looks similar to kale.*

Thai mixed vegetable curry

3 small red onions, peeled and sliced

3 garlic cloves, peeled and crushed

2 tablespoons Thai Red Curry Paste (see page 45)

500 g / 1 lb 2 oz mixed vegetables, such as green beans, courgettes, mushrooms, Chinese greens, Thai kale, broccoli florets, cauliflower florets

500 g / 1 lb 2 oz firm tofu, cut into bite-sized pieces

600 ml / 1 pint vegetable stock

400 ml can coconut milk

juice of ½ lime

vegetable oil, for frying

1 Heat some oil in a heavy-based pan and fry the onions until they are softened and lightly browned.

2 Add the garlic and cook for about 1 minute, then add the curry paste and stir-fry for about 1 minute.

3 Add the vegetables and stir-fry until they are slightly softened, then add the tofu and stir-fry until it is coated in the curry mixture.

4 Add all the remaining ingredients and simmer, stirring regularly, for 7–10 minutes.

5 Serve with plain boiled rice.

Vegetables in coconut milk

2 garlic cloves, peeled and finely
    chopped
5 cm/2 inch piece fresh root ginger,
    peeled and grated
2 teaspoons pickled green peppercorns,
    rinsed
1 aubergine, topped and tailed and cut
    into bite-sized cubes
1 small sweet potato, peeled and cut into
    bite-sized chunks
100 g/3½ oz green beans, cut into
    5 cm/2 inch pieces
8 or 10 thin asparagus spears, cut into
    5 cm/2 inch pieces
150 ml/5 fl oz coconut milk
a good handful of baby spinach leaves
a handful of fresh basil leaves
2 teaspoons Thai fish sauce (nam pla)
vegetable or coconut oil, for frying

1 Heat some oil in a wok or heavy-based frying pan and stir-fry the garlic, ginger and peppercorns for about 30 seconds.

2 Add the aubergine, sweet potato and a dash of water and stir-fry for about 5 minutes.

3 Add the beans, cover and cook for 4–5 minutes, shaking the wok or pan every so often to prevent the vegetables from sticking.

4 Add the asparagus and coconut milk and cook for 3–4 minutes.

5 Stir in the spinach, basil and fish sauce and cook until the leaves have just started to wilt. Serve hot.

Steamed sweetcorn

5 cm/2 inch piece fresh root ginger,
    peeled and grated
3 garlic cloves, peeled and finely
    chopped
1 large, fresh red chilli, deseeded and
    finely chopped
2 teaspoons pickled green peppercorns,
    rinsed and crushed
2 tablespoons water
4 frozen corn cobs, cut into about
    7.5 cm/3 inch lengths
2 tablespoons Thai fish sauce (nam pla)

1 In a small bowl, mix the ginger with the garlic, chilli, peppercorns and water.

2 Press the mixture onto the corn cobs and place in a bamboo steamer lined with greaseproof paper.

3 Place the steamer over a wok or pan of boiling water, cover and steam for about 20 minutes, or until the corn is tender.

4 Sprinkle with the fish sauce and serve.

Fish and shellfish

Above left to right *An array of dried and smoked fish at Klong Toey Market. Cooking mussels in a restaurant at Samut Sakhon, on the Tha Chin Klong river. The beginnings of a green prawn curry.*

Fish and shellfish

Gimme some seafood, mama

The Thais, along with the Spanish and the Japanese, must be among the most enthusiastic consumers of fish. From the cool streams and rivers in the North comes an abundance of freshwater fish. The warm waters of the Gulf of Thailand and the Andaman Sea are packed with a scintillating variety of fish, from squid, crabs, lobsters, prawns, shrimp, scallops and oysters to groupers, mullets, sea perch, John Dory, kingfish, catfish and bass; the piscatorial menu is endless. Then there are cockles, clams and mussels – virtually everything that swims in the sea is edible. But I still can't face 'sea cucumbers', those awful, large, transparent sea slugs!

Despite what is specified in my recipes, you can use whatever fish you like. If, for example, you are deep-frying a whole bass, leave its head and tail on, but gut it and cut off its fins.

Shrimps and prawns, throughout this book, in most instances, should be green tiger prawns, fresh or frozen, but definitely raw. Leave on their heads and tails, but take off their shells. Run a sharp knife down the centre of the back and remove the black intestinal cord; this incision will make the prawn, whether steamed, fried or deep-fried, 'butterfly' into a pretty shape when cooked.

We do not all have the luxury of being able to buy fresh fish from the trawler, the line or the sea on our doorstep, but as far as possible please try to buy fresh fish. The eyes should not be glazed, milky or cloudy, they should be bright like jewels. Lift up the gills and see that they are fresh and clean underneath. Make sure that the flesh is always firm to the prod, to the squeeze or to the touch; and finally, fresh fish does not smell of fish – it smells of beautiful fresh salt or fresh water.

King scallops baked in rice wine

2 tablespoons unsalted butter
2 tablespoons rice wine
4 garlic cloves, peeled
1 teaspoon sliced coriander root
10 peppercorns
¼ teaspoon salt
300 g / 11 oz large, raw scallops, corals
    attached

1 Preheat the oven to 180°C / 350°F / gas mark 4. Melt the butter in a saucepan, then stir in the rice wine.

2 Using a pestle and mortar or spice grinder, grind the garlic, coriander root, peppercorns and salt together to make a paste.

3 Arrange the scallops in a greased, ovenproof dish, top with the paste mixture and pour a little of the butter and rice wine mixture over each one.

4 Bake in the oven for a few minutes until they sizzle and the garlic is turning brown. Serve hot.

Chargrilled crab or lobster

2 fat crabs or lobsters, each weighing
    300–400 g / 11–14 oz
7 garlic cloves, peeled and finely chopped
5 small, fresh, hot red chillies, finely
    chopped
1 tablespoon lime juice
1 tablespoon Thai fish sauce (nam pla)

1 Wash the crabs or lobsters and place on a hot charcoal grill or barbeque until red all over and cooked.

2 Remove the shell (and the stomach sac and gills in the case of the crab, these you discard) and chop into pieces. In either case, crack the claws. Arrange on a serving dish.

3 In a spice grinder, whiz the garlic, chillies, lime juice and fish sauce to serve with the crab or lobster, or use any other dipping sauce of your choice (see pages 51–57).

Above *All sorts of wonderful prawns at the market.*

Green prawns steamed with soy sauce

4 garlic cloves, peeled and finely
    chopped
1 tablespoon fresh coriander roots, finely
    chopped
2 tablespoons light soy sauce
1 teaspoon oyster sauce
10 large, raw tiger prawns, shelled and
    deveined (see page 145)
2 red shallots, peeled and finely chopped
freshly ground black pepper, to taste

1 In a small bowl, mix the garlic with the coriander roots, soy sauce and oyster sauce and pour over the prawns.

2 Arrange the prawns on a plate and place in a steamer set over boiling water, then steam for 5–6 minutes until the prawns have turned pink.

3 Place the prawns on a serving dish and sprinkle with the shallots and black pepper. Serve hot.

Green prawn curry

400 ml can coconut milk

6 tablespoons water

2 tablespoons Thai Green Curry Paste
(see page 45)

6 kaffir lime leaves, or 1 tablespoon
lime zest

100 g / 3½ oz French beans, cut into
2.5 cm / 1 inch pieces

500 g / 1 lb 2 oz large, raw tiger prawns,
head and shell removed but tail left
on, and deveined (see page 145)

2 tablespoons Thai fish sauce (nam pla)

2 tablespoons lime juice

grated zest of 1 lime

1 teaspoon pickled green peppercorns,
rinsed and drained

2 teaspoons soft brown sugar

a handful each of fresh coriander and
basil leaves, to garnish

1 In a large pan, heat the coconut milk and water for
about 5 minutes, or until the oil from the coconut milk
begins to separate.

2 Add the curry paste, lime leaves or zest and the beans
to the pan and bring the heat up to simmering point.
Simmer for about 10 minutes.

3 Add the prawns to the pan and simmer for about
5 minutes, or until the prawns have turned pink.

4 Add the fish sauce, lime juice and zest, green
peppercorns and sugar and stir gently to mix all the
ingredients.

5 Garnish with the coriander and basil leaves and
serve hot.

Opposite *Getting stuck into the green prawn curry.*
Below *A calm backwater at the Damnoen-Saduak floating market.*

Prawn and pineapple curry

185 ml/6½ fl oz coconut milk

300 g/11 oz fresh pineapple, peeled,
    eyes and core removed, and cut into
    small chunks

2 tablespoons tamarind paste

3 kaffir lime leaves, or ½ tablespoon
    lime zest

250 g/9 oz raw tiger prawns, shelled and
    deveined (see page 145)

2 teaspoons Thai fish sauce (nam pla)

1 tablespoon Demerara or palm sugar

vegetable oil, for frying

For the paste

4 red bird's eye chillies, deseeded

6 red shallots, peeled and chopped

2 fresh lemon grass stalks, chopped

½ teaspoon shrimp paste

1 teaspoon turmeric powder

1 Put all the ingredients for the paste into a spice grinder and grind to a paste (add a little water if the mixture is a bit stiff).

2 Heat a little oil in a wok or heavy-based pan, add the paste and stir-fry for a minute or so until the fragrance is released.

3 Add the coconut milk and cook for a couple of minutes, then add the pineapple chunks, tamarind paste and lime leaves or zest and simmer for 5–7 minutes.

4 Add the prawns and simmer for another 5 minutes until the prawns have turned pink and are cooked through. Just before serving stir in the fish sauce and sugar.

Stir-fried garlic prawns

1 tablespoon light soy sauce

1½ tablespoons oyster sauce

½ teaspoon Demerara or palm sugar

18 fresh coriander roots, chopped

10 black peppercorns

5 garlic cloves, peeled and chopped

500 g/1 lb 2 oz large, raw tiger prawns,
    shelled and deveined (see page 145)

1 large, fresh red chilli, deseeded and
    finely sliced

vegetable oil, for frying

a handful of fresh coriander leaves,
    chopped, to garnish

1 In a small bowl, mix the soy and oyster sauces with the sugar and set aside.

2 Put the coriander roots, peppercorns and garlic into a small food processor and whiz to a paste.

3 Stir-fry the paste in a little oil in a wok or heavy-based frying pan for a minute or so, until it releases its fragrance. Add the prawns, sliced chilli and soy sauce mixture and stir-fry for a couple of minutes or so, or until the prawns turn pink.

4 Place on a serving dish and garnish with the chopped coriander.

Above *Trimming prawns can be rather monotonous.*

Prawn omelette

3 garlic cloves, peeled and finely
    chopped

2 fresh lemon grass stalks, finely
    chopped

2 fresh coriander roots, finely chopped

1 medium, fresh red chilli, deseeded and
    finely chopped

500 g / 1 lb 2 oz small, raw prawns,
    shelled

3 spring onions, trimmed and chopped

1 tablespoon Thai fish sauce (nam pla)

2 teaspoons soft brown sugar

4 eggs

2 tablespoons water

freshly ground black pepper, to taste

vegetable oil, for frying

chopped fresh coriander leaves, to
    garnish

1 Heat a little oil in a wok or heavy-based frying pan, add the garlic, lemon grass, coriander roots and chilli and stir-fry for 20–30 seconds.

2 Add the prawns and stir-fry until the prawns turn pink.

3 Add the spring onions, half the fish sauce, the sugar and black pepper and mix well, then remove from the pan and set aside to keep warm.

4 To make the omelette, beat together the eggs, water and remaining fish sauce until the mixture is fluffy.

5 Heat a little oil in the wok or frying pan and pour in the egg mixture, swirling the mixture around until the bottom of the pan is coated. Using a fork, keep pulling in the sides of the egg mixture and filling up the gaps with uncooked egg until all the omelette is set.

6 Tip the omelette flat onto a warmed plate, spoon the prawn mixture into the centre and fold the edges of the omelette over the prawns.

7 Garnish with the chopped coriander and serve.

Mussels steamed with lemon grass

450 g / 1 lb mussels in their shells,
   debearded and scrubbed
3 garlic cloves, peeled and finely chopped
1 red onion, peeled and finely chopped
2.5 cm / 1 inch piece fresh root ginger,
   peeled and finely chopped
3 fresh lemon grass stalks, finely sliced
   into rings
2 large, fresh red chillies, deseeded and
   finely chopped, plus sliced chillies to
   garnish
1 tablespoon Thai fish sauce (nam pla)
juice of 1 lime
½ teaspoon Demerara or palm sugar
vegetable oil, for frying

1 Wash the mussels in several changes of cold water to ensure all the sand and grit have been removed. Throw away any mussels that do not close fully when gently tapped.

2 Heat a little oil in a wok and stir-fry the garlic, onion, ginger, lemon grass and chillies gently for a couple of minutes until they release their fragrance.

3 Tip the mussels into the wok and stir-fry for a couple of minutes.

4 Add the fish sauce, lime juice and sugar, cover with a lid and cook for about 5 minutes, shaking the pan at intervals until the mussels are all open.

5 Discard any mussels that are still closed and serve hot garnished with sliced chillies.

Opposite *Mussels steamed with lemon grass*

Steamed fish curry

In rural areas of Thailand, the mixture would be placed in banana leaves, lightly tied up and then steamed.

2 tablespoons chilli paste
2 teaspoons Thai fish sauce (nam pla)
250 ml can coconut cream
100 g / 3½ oz raw tiger prawns, shelled
   and deveined (see page 145)
100 g / 3½ oz squid, cleaned and cut into
   bite-sized pieces
100 g / 3½ oz raw white crab meat
100 g / 3½ oz monkfish fillets, membranes
   removed and cut into bite-sized pieces
½ white cabbage, shredded
a good handful of basil leaves
1 tablespoon finely shredded kaffir lime
   leaves, or ½ tablespoon lime zest
3 large, fresh red chillies, deseeded and
   finely sliced

1 Place the chilli paste, fish sauce and three-quarters of the coconut cream in a bowl and mix well.

2 Add the prawns, squid, crab meat and monkfish and mix well, then leave aside for 10–15 minutes for the flavours to develop.

3 Make a bed of the cabbage and basil leaves in a large bowl and pour on the seafood and fish mixture.

4 Pour over the remaining coconut cream, the lime leaves or zest and the sliced chillies, then put the bowl in a steamer and steam over a high heat for about 15 minutes until the fish is cooked. Serve hot.

Peppers stuffed with curried fish

275 g / 10 oz firm white fish fillets, cut
    into 1 cm / ½ inch pieces
2 eggs
400 ml can coconut milk
2 tablespoons Thai fish sauce (nam pla)

For the curry paste
2 large, fresh red chillies, chopped
3 garlic cloves, peeled and chopped
2 red shallots, peeled and chopped
4 fresh coriander roots, finely chopped
1 fresh lemon grass stalk, chopped
1 cm / ½ inch piece fresh root ginger,
    peeled and finely chopped
2 kaffir lime leaves, finely shredded,
    or zest of ½ lime
1 teaspoon shrimp paste
salt, to taste

For the peppers
4 peppers, red and green, cut in half,
    deseeded and pith removed
2 tablespoons coconut cream

To garnish
1 large red chilli, deseeded and finely
    sliced
zest of 2 limes

1 Place all the ingredients for the curry paste in a blender and whiz to a paste.

2 To make the fish curry filling, put the curry paste in a bowl, stir in the fish, eggs, coconut milk and fish sauce and put in the fridge for 30 minutes.

3 To prepare the peppers, place the halved peppers on a plate, fill each one with some of the fish mixture and place the plate in a steamer set over a pan of simmering water. Steam for about 15 minutes or so.

4 When they are cooked, place the peppers on a serving dish, drizzle on a little coconut cream and sprinkle on the sliced chilli and the lime zest as a garnish.

Right These colourful fishing boats are at Sri-racha, a district in Chonburi Province, east of Bangkok. **Opposite** *The fish market.*

Seafood steamboat or hotpot

If you do not have a Thai steamboat, you could use a fondue set for this dish.

900 ml / 1½ pints fish or chicken stock

½ head of greens, such as green
cabbage or spring greens, shredded

1 stringed celery stick, cut into bite-sized
pieces

400 g / 14 oz large, raw tiger prawns,
shelled and deveined (see page 145)

200 g / 7 oz sea perch fillets, cut into bite-
sized pieces (or use sea bream, sea
bass or any firm white fish, or prawns)

200 g / 7 oz squid, cleaned and cut into
bite-sized pieces

200 g / 7 oz scallops

1 carrot, peeled and cut into very fine strips

For the dipping sauce

1 tablespoon fermented soybeans

1 tablespoon minced fresh coriander root

4 garlic cloves, peeled and crushed

3 large red chillies, finely chopped

juice of 2 limes

5 tablespoons Thai fish sauce (nam pla)

1 teaspoon light soy sauce

1 teaspoon Demerara or palm sugar

1 Mix all the ingredients for the dipping sauce in a bowl, then pour into small bowls and put to one side.

2 Heat the stock in the steamboat or fondue pan to a slow rolling boil, then add the greens and celery.

3 Place all the fish, seafood and carrot on a serving dish in the middle of the table, with the bowls of dipping sauce.

4 Each diner places a piece of fish and carrot into the steamboat to cook and then dips it into the sauce. The stock is then had as a soup.

Above *A brother and sister fish on the river at Karasin, northeastern province.*

Deep-fried fish with sweet and sour sauce

400 g / 14 oz John Dory, sea bream, red
    snapper or red mullet, gutted, cleaned
    and scaled
3 tablespoons plain flour
225 g / 8 oz can pineapple chunks in its
    own juice (drain the chunks and
    reserve the juice)
1½ tablespoons plum sauce
2 teaspoons Thai fish sauce (nam pla)
1 tablespoon soft brown sugar
4 garlic cloves, peeled and finely
    chopped
1 red onion, peeled and sliced
½ red pepper, deseeded and pith
    removed, cut into chunks
½ cucumber, deseeded but skin left on,
    cut into chunks
6 cherry tomatoes
freshly ground black pepper, to taste
vegetable oil, for frying
a handful of fresh coriander leaves,
    chopped, to garnish

1 Cut 3 or 4 deep slashes on each side of whichever fish you have chosen.

2 Season 2 tablespoons of the flour with the black pepper. Dip the fish in the seasoned flour to coat both sides, then shake off the excess.

3 Heat enough oil for deep-frying in a deep pan to a medium heat, then lower the fish into the hot oil and cook for 12–15 minutes until lightly browned. Remove the fish from the pan, shake off any excess oil and drain on kitchen paper. Leave aside in a warm place.

4 Meanwhile, mix the pineapple juice with the plum sauce, fish sauce, sugar and the remaining flour until you have a smooth mixture.

5 In another pan, heat a little oil and stir-fry the garlic briefly until just turning brown, then add the onion and red pepper and stir-fry for another minute or so. Add the pineapple chunks, cucumber, tomatoes and pineapple juice mixture.

6 Continue to stir-fry until the mixture starts to thicken and the flour is cooked, then pour over the fried fish and garnish with the chopped coriander.

Deep-fried fish with chillies and basil

3 tablespoons plain flour

1 large fish, such as bass, bream or
    mullet, gutted, cleaned and scaled

a good handful of fresh basil leaves

2 dried red chillies, deseeded and cut
    into rings

freshly ground black pepper, to taste

vegetable oil, for frying

3 kaffir lime leaves, finely sliced, or
    $\frac{1}{2}$ tablespoon lime zest, to garnish

For the sauce

$\frac{1}{2}$ tablespoon Thai Red Curry Paste (see
    page 45)

2 tablespoons Demerara or palm sugar

2 tablespoons Thai fish sauce (nam pla)

1 Place the flour on a plate and season with black pepper. Dip the fish fillets in the flour to coat both sides, then shake off any excess.

2 To make the sauce, heat some oil in a wok or heavy-based frying pan and stir-fry the curry paste for a minute or two, then add the sugar, fish sauce and a little water and cook for a couple more minutes. Remove from the heat and set aside.

3 Heat more oil in a large pan and deep-fry the basil leaves in two batches for about 1 minute each batch until they are crispy. Using a slotted spoon, remove and drain on kitchen paper. Deep-fry the chillies for about 30 seconds, then remove and drain on kitchen paper.

4 Using the same oil, deep-fry the fish fillets for 5–7 minutes until the fish is browned and cooked, then drain on kitchen paper and keep warm on a serving dish.

5 Reheat the sauce and pour over the fish. Scatter the fried basil leaves and chillies on top, garnish with the lime leaves or zest and serve.

Fried John Dory with shrimps and mango

400–500 g / 14 oz–1 lb 2 oz John Dory,
    gutted, cleaned and scaled

2 tablespoons Thai fish sauce (nam pla)

2 tablespoons cornflour

$\frac{1}{2}$ green mango, shredded

2 red shallots, peeled and finely sliced

1 tablespoon ground, dried shrimp

1 small, fresh red chilli, deseeded and
    finely sliced

1 teaspoon Demerara or palm sugar

$\frac{1}{4}$ white cabbage, shredded

5 dried hot chillies, fried in oil for 2 minutes

vegetable oil, for frying

1 Cut the fillets off the John Dory and rub them with a few drops of fish sauce. Coat them in the cornflour on both sides, then shake off any excess.

2 Heat some oil in a wok or heavy-based frying pan and shallow-fry the fillets on both sides until golden brown, then remove from the pan, drain on kitchen paper and keep warm.

3 In a bowl, mix the mango with the shallots, shrimp and sliced chilli, then add the sugar and remaining fish sauce, or to taste.

4 Arrange the mango mixture on the plate with the fish and serve the shredded cabbage and hot fried chillies alongside.

Bass with chilli and lime sauce

1 tablespoon cornflour

6 medium-sized firm bass fillets

6 garlic cloves, peeled and crushed

2 fresh red chillies, deseeded and finely
    chopped

1 tablespoon soft brown sugar

juice of 2 limes

grated zest of 1 lime

2 tablespoons water

vegetable oil, for frying

1 Place the cornflour on a plate and dip the fish fillets in the flour to coat both sides. Shake off any excess.

2 Heat some oil in a wok or heavy-based frying pan and fry the fillets on both sides in batches of two until they are golden brown. Drain each batch on kitchen paper and keep them warm while you fry the remainder.

3 In the same pan, stir-fry the garlic and chillies for 2 minutes. Add the sugar, lime juice and zest and the water and bring the sauce to the boil, then cook for another minute, stirring all the time.

4 Spoon over the fish and serve.

Fried minced prawn and pork in seaweed rolls

150 g / 5 oz raw tiger prawns, shelled,
    deveined (see page 145) and minced

100 g / 3½ oz minced pork

½ teaspoon Demerara or palm sugar

1 sheet dried seaweed

4 leaves pak choi, shredded

salt and freshly ground black pepper,
    to taste

vegetable oil, for frying

To garnish

a handful of fresh coriander leaves

1 fresh red chilli, deseeded and thinly
    sliced

1 Mix the minced prawns and pork together with your hands, then mix in the sugar, salt and black pepper. Spread the mixture over the surface of the sheet of seaweed to 1 cm / ½ inch thick and roll up into a long roll.

2 Heat some oil in a wok or heavy-based frying pan to a medium heat and fry the roll, turning, for about 8 minutes or so. Remove from the oil and cut into small rolls.

3 Fry the pak choi until crisp, then remove from the pan and drain on kitchen paper.

4 Spread the pak choi on a serving dish and top with the seaweed rolls. Garnish each roll with a coriander leaf and a sprinkling of sliced chilli.

Opposite top *This delightful waterfront restaurant, the Bangkoknoi, was on the Chao Phraya River.* Opposite bottom *In their kitchens I cooked a sea bass in the same style as the bass with chilli and lime sauce above, although I cooked the fish whole.*

Meat and poultry

Above left to right *Broiled ducks at the Pet-Palo-Huahaheng Duck Restaurant. Chilli oil. One of the many restaurants and eating places in Chatuchak Market.*

Meat and poultry
Gorgeous pigs, fat ducks, buffaloes and squawking, long-legged chickens

My grandmother Kate kept a pig. She had a larder full of bacon, ham, knuckles, pickles and preserves. My grandfather, Harold, kept chickens. My father grew runner beans and repaired watches, while my mother made chutneys, jams and pickles.

On Sundays my grandfather, still wearing his leather apron – he was a cobbler – would stump around the garden on his tin leg, which replaced the leg that he had lost in the Battle of the

Somme, during the First World War, and, with knife in hand, would murder a bird. By the way, on rainy Saturday nights, he would collect snails from the privet hedge and bake them on a shovel on the coal fire. But back to Sundays: he would slash the chicken's head with one clean, fast cut and the chicken would run on and on until the pulsating blood pumped out its life.

You will see worse in the East, but you will eat better. Birds and beasts are born to be wild and eaten.

P.S. In Thailand my beef recipes would be prepared with buffalo, chewy but toothsome!

And, to mix all my culinary metaphors and philosophy, Confuscious said: 'Give a man a fish and he will live for a day. But, teach a man to fish and he will live forever.' However, Floyd says: 'Teach a man to eat and only then can you teach him how to cook.'

Caramelised pork

4 red shallots, peeled and finely sliced
5 garlic cloves, peeled and finely
    chopped
500 g / 1 lb 2 oz pork fillet, cut into thin
    slices
1 tablespoon light soy sauce
1 tablespoon oyster sauce
1 tablespoon Thai fish sauce (nam pla)
4 tablespoons palm or soft brown sugar
a pinch of ground white pepper
vegetable oil, for deep-frying

1 Heat enough oil for deep-frying in a wok or deep saucepan and deep-fry the shallots over a medium heat until they are crispy and golden. Remove from the oil, drain on kitchen paper and put to one side.

2 Drain off most of the oil to leave 1–2 tablespoons and stir-fry the garlic until just turning golden.

3 Add the pork and stir-fry for about 3 minutes, then add the soy sauce, oyster sauce, fish sauce, sugar and white pepper and continue cooking for about 5 minutes. The dish is cooked when the sauce has thickened and becomes sticky, coating the pork.

4 Serve sprinkled with the crispy fried shallots sprinkled on top.

Stir-fried pork with ginger

15 g / ½ oz Chinese dried black
    mushrooms, soaked in warm water for
    20 minutes
3 garlic cloves, peeled and finely chopped
500 g / 1 lb 2 oz pork fillet, finely sliced
1 red onion, peeled and cut into 8 wedges
5 cm / 2 inch piece fresh root ginger,
    peeled and cut into fine matchsticks
2 spring onions, trimmed and cut in half
    lengthways, then in 5 cm / 2 inch pieces
vegetable oil, for frying

For the sauce
4 tablespoons chicken stock
1 tablespoon Thai fish sauce (nam pla)
2 tablespoons oyster sauce
½ teaspoon Demerara or palm sugar

To garnish
1 large, fresh red chilli, deseeded and cut
    in strips
a handful of fresh coriander leaves,
    chopped

1 Drain and dry the mushrooms, discard the stems and cut into slices.

2 Mix all the ingredients for the sauce in a small bowl and put to one side.

3 Heat some oil in a wok or heavy-based frying pan and stir-fry half the garlic until just turning golden.

4 Increase the heat and add half the pork slices, then stir-fry for 2–3 minutes. Remove from the wok and repeat the process with the remaining garlic and pork.

5 Return all the garlic and pork to the wok, add the mushrooms, red onion and ginger and stir well. Add the sauce mixture and stir-fry for a minute or two.

6 Just before serving, add the spring onions and toss well with the other ingredients. Turn out onto a serving dish and garnish with the chilli and chopped coriander.

Above *This young lady has her hands full.*

Stir-fried pork with green beans

3–4 garlic cloves, peeled and finely
    chopped
250 g/9 oz pork fillet, finely sliced
250 g/9 oz French green beans, cut into
    5 cm/2 inch pieces
vegetable oil, for frying
1 large, fresh red chilli, deseeded and
    shredded, to garnish

For the sauce
1 tablespoon oyster sauce
1 tablespoon light soy sauce
½ teaspoon Demerara or palm sugar
2 tablespoons water

1 Mix all the ingredients for the sauce in a small bowl
and put to one side.

2 Heat some oil in a wok or heavy-based frying pan and
stir-fry the garlic until just turning golden.

3 Add the pork slices and stir-fry for 4–5 minutes, or until
the pork is cooked.

4 Add the beans and the sauce and stir-fry for another
4–5 minutes.

5 Tip onto a serving dish, garnish with the shredded chilli
and serve.

Red pork curry

60 ml / 2½ fl oz coconut cream
2 tablespoons Thai Red Curry Paste (see
     page 45)
1½ tablespoons Demerara or palm sugar
3 tablespoons Thai fish sauce (nam pla)
500 g / 1 lb 2 oz pork fillet, finely sliced
450 ml / 15 fl oz coconut milk
1 aubergine, topped and tailed and cut
     into cubes
75 g / 3 oz pickled green peppercorns,
     rinsed and drained
6 kaffir lime leaves, shredded, or
     1 tablespoon lime zest
2 large, fresh red chillies, deseeded and
     shredded

1 Pour the coconut cream into a wok or heavy-based frying pan and simmer, stirring, for about 5 minutes until the oil separates from the cream.

2 Add the curry paste and combine well, then cook for a couple of minutes until the paste gives off its fragrance.

3 Add the sugar and fish sauce and cook until the mixture turns a darker colour, then add the pork slices and cook, stirring, for another 6–7 minutes.

4 Add the coconut milk and simmer for 5 minutes.

5 Add the aubergine and peppercorns and cook for another 5 minutes.

6 Add the lime leaves or zest and cook for 1 minute, then transfer to a serving dish. Garnish with the shredded chillies and serve with steamed rice.

Below *Green peppercorns*

Chiang Mai pork curry

500 g / 1 lb 2 oz pork belly, cut into bite-sized cubes
2 garlic cloves, peeled and finely chopped
2 tablespoons Chiang Mai Curry Paste (see page 48)
4 red shallots, peeled and quartered
5 cm / 2 inch piece fresh root ginger, peeled and shredded
3 tablespoons unsalted roasted peanuts, chopped
500 ml / 17 fl oz water
3 tablespoons tamarind paste
2 tablespoons Thai fish sauce (nam pla)
2 tablespoons Demerara or palm sugar
vegetable oil, for frying

1 Blanch the cubes of pork in boiling water for 1 minute, then drain and dry them.

2 Heat some oil in a wok or heavy-based saucepan and stir-fry the garlic for 1 minute, or until turning golden.

3 Add the curry paste and stir-fry for a couple of minutes until it releases its fragrance.

4 Add the pork, shallots, ginger and peanuts and stir to mix well, then add the water and tamarind paste and bring the mixture to the boil.

5 Add the fish sauce and sugar, reduce the heat and simmer for about 1½ hours or until the pork is tender. Check the dish during the cooking and add more water if necessary.

6 When the pork is very tender the dish is ready.

Stir-fried beef with basil leaves

4 garlic cloves, peeled and finely chopped
500 g / 1 lb 2 oz fillet steak, thinly sliced
3 dried bird's eye chillies, crushed
1 red onion, peeled and cut into thin wedges
2 handfuls of fresh basil leaves
vegetable oil, for frying

For the sauce
4 tablespoons chicken stock
1 tablespoon Thai fish sauce (nam pla)
2 tablespoons oyster sauce
½ teaspoon Demerara or palm sugar

1 Mix all the ingredients for the sauce in a small bowl and put to one side.

2 Heat some oil in a wok or heavy-based frying pan and stir-fry half the garlic until just turning golden.

3 Increase the heat, add half the beef and half the chillies and stir-fry for 2–3 minutes until the beef is cooked. Using a slotted spoon, remove the garlic, beef and chillies and set aside, then repeat the process with the remaining garlic, beef and chillies.

4 Return all the beef, chillies and garlic to the wok. Add the onion and the sauce mixture and stir-fry for a minute or so.

5 Throw in the basil leaves and stir round until the leaves begin to wilt, then tip onto a serving dish.

Above *Farmer's son Aye on a bolting buffalo.*

Massaman beef curry

5 cloves

10 cardamom pods

2 cinnamon sticks

2 tablespoons Thai Massaman Curry
Paste (see page 46)

800 g / 1 lb 12 oz rump steak, cut into
5 cm / 2 inch cubes

400 ml can coconut milk

250 ml / 8½ fl oz beef stock

3 potatoes, peeled and cut into 2.5 cm /
1 inch cubes

2.5 cm / 1 inch piece fresh root ginger,
peeled and shredded

3 tablespoons Thai fish sauce (nam pla)

3 tablespoons Demerara or palm sugar

3 tablespoons tamarind paste

100 g / 3½ oz unsalted roasted peanuts,
chopped

vegetable oil, for frying

1 Heat a wok or heavy-based frying pan and dry-roast
the cloves, cardamom pods and cinnamon sticks over a
low heat, stirring for 40–50 seconds until they release
their fragrance. Remove from the pan and set aside.

2 Heat some oil in the same wok or pan and stir-fry the
curry paste for a couple of minutes. Add the beef and
stir-fry for about 5 minutes.

3 Add the coconut milk, stock, potatoes, ginger, fish
sauce, sugar, tamarind paste, dry-fried spices and two-
thirds of the peanuts. Reduce the heat and simmer
gently for about 1 hour or until the meat is very tender
and the potatoes are cooked.

4 Serve sprinkled with the remaining peanuts.

Above *Some magnificent Buddhas at a wat near Karasin, northeastern province.*

Penang beef curry

2 tablespoons Penang Curry Paste (see
    page 47)
700 g / 1 lb 8 oz flank or sirloin beef or
    buffalo flank steak, cut into thin strips
185 ml / 6 ½ fl oz coconut milk
1 tablespoon Demerara or palm sugar
3 tablespoons tamarind paste
1 tablespoon Thai fish sauce (nam pla)
vegetable oil, for frying

To garnish

3 kaffir lime leaves, finely sliced, or
    ½ tablespoon lime zest
1 large, fresh red chilli, deseeded and
    finely sliced

1 Heat some oil in a wok or heavy-based frying pan and stir-fry the curry paste for about 2 minutes until it releases its fragrance.

2 Add the beef or buffalo and stir-fry for 5–6 minutes.

3 Add three-quarters of the coconut milk, the sugar, tamarind paste and fish sauce, reduce the heat and simmer gently for 5–6 minutes. If the mixture is looking too dry, add a little water.

4 Spoon into a serving dish, pour over the remaining coconut milk and sprinkle with the lime leaves or zest and the sliced chilli.

Above left to right *The meat section at Klong Toey Market, where they sell these very handy charcoal-burners.*

Dried fillet steak with chilli sauce

350 g / 12 oz fillet steak, cut into 1 cm /
½ inch strips
vegetable oil, for deep-frying (optional)
Thai Sweet Chilli Sauce (see page 51), to
serve

For the marinade
2 teaspoons coriander seeds
1 teaspoon cumin seeds
1 bunch of fresh coriander roots, finely
chopped
4 garlic cloves, peeled and finely
chopped
1 teaspoon white peppercorns
a pinch of salt
2 tablespoons Demerara or palm sugar
2 tablespoons soy sauce

1 To make the marinade, heat a wok or heavy-based frying pan and dry-roast the coriander and cumin seeds for 40–50 seconds until they release their fragrance. Using a spice grinder or pestle and mortar, grind together the coriander and cumin seeds, the coriander roots, garlic, peppercorns and salt. Turn this out into a bowl, add the sugar and soy sauce and mix to form a marinade.

2 Tip the steak into this mixture, mix well to coat on both sides, then cover and leave in the refrigerator overnight.

3 Remove the steak from the marinade. Preheat the oven to its lowest setting and lay the steak strips on a cooling rack. Place in the oven and leave for about 4 hours until they are dry and quite hard.

4 If the beef has not 'crisped up', heat about 5 cm / 2 inches oil in a wok or heavy-based frying pan to a high temperature, drop in the beef strips in batches and fry until crispy. Remove with a slotted spoon and drain on kitchen paper.

5 Serve immediately with a bowl of chilli sauce for dipping.

Red duck curry

750 ml/1¼ pints coconut milk
250 ml/8½ fl oz coconut cream
1 small roasted duck, jointed
3 tablespoons Thai Red Curry Paste (see
    page 45)
2 tablespoons Thai fish sauce (nam pla)
1 tablespoon Demerara or palm sugar
1 small aubergine, topped and tailed and
    cut into 1 cm/½ inch cubes
4 kaffir lime leaves, torn, or zest of 1 lime
2 fresh red chillies, sliced diagonally
a handful of fresh basil leaves

1 Pour the coconut milk and coconut cream into a deep pan and bring to the boil. Reduce the heat to a simmer, add the duck joints and simmer for about 10 minutes (if the mixture looks too thick and oily, add some water).

2 Skim off about 1 tablespoon of the coconut oil that has formed and heat it in a wok or heavy-based frying pan. Fry the curry paste in this oil for about 2 minutes, adding a little more of the original coconut liquid to loosen the mixture. Season with the fish sauce and sugar and stir until the sugar has dissolved.

3 Tip this curry mixture into the coconut and duck, add the aubergine and simmer for 5 minutes. Then add the lime leaves or zest, the chillies and basil and the dish is ready to serve.

Green chicken curry

4 red shallots, peeled and sliced
2 tablespoons Thai Green Curry Paste
    (see page 45)
60 ml/2½ fl oz coconut cream
350 g/12 oz skinless chicken breast
    fillets, sliced into 1 cm/½ inch strips
450 ml/15 fl oz coconut milk
2 tablespoons Thai fish sauce (nam pla)
1 tablespoon Demerara or palm sugar
1 aubergine, topped and tailed and cut
    into 2.5 cm/1 inch pieces
2.5 cm/1 inch piece fresh root ginger,
    peeled and finely chopped
7 kaffir lime leaves, torn in half, or
    1 tablespoon lime zest
1 teaspoon pickled green peppercorns,
    rinsed and drained
a handful of fresh basil leaves
1 large, fresh red chilli, deseeded and
    shredded
vegetable oil, for frying

1 Heat some oil in a wok or heavy-based frying pan and stir-fry the shallots for about 1 minute.

2 Add the curry paste and stir-fry for about 2 minutes, then add the coconut cream and cook, stirring, for about 3 minutes.

3 Add the chicken and cook, stirring, for 2 minutes, then add nearly all the coconut milk (save a little for serving), the fish sauce and sugar and simmer over a medium heat for about 5 minutes.

4 Add the aubergine and continue to simmer, stirring occasionally, for 6–7 minutes until the aubergine is cooked.

5 Add the ginger, lime leaves or zest, the peppercorns and basil and cook for another minute or so. Transfer to serving bowls and sprinkle over the remaining coconut milk and the shredded chilli.

Opposite *The pace was fast and furious in the kitchens of the Intercontinental Hotel.*

Yellow curry with chicken

4 red shallots, peeled and sliced
2 tablespoons Thai Yellow Curry Paste
    (see page 46)
4 tablespoons coconut cream
500 g / 1 lb 2 oz skinless chicken breast
    fillets, cut into 2.5 cm / 1 inch strips
400 ml can coconut milk
1 tablespoon Thai fish sauce (nam pla)
2 teaspoons Demerara or palm sugar
2 small sweet potatoes, peeled, cubed
    and partly boiled
vegetable oil, for frying

*Opposite Aye survived his ride on the runaway
buffalo and is reunited with his chicken.*

1 Heat some oil in a wok or heavy-based frying pan and stir-fry the shallots until they are crispy. Using a slotted spoon, remove from the wok and drain on kitchen paper, then set aside.

2 Using the same oil, stir-fry the curry paste for a couple of minutes until it releases its fragrance.

3 Add the coconut cream and mix well, then bring to a simmer, add the chicken and leave to cook for about 5 minutes (don't stir this mixture).

4 Add the coconut milk, fish sauce and sugar and cook for about 5 minutes until the chicken is cooked. Using a slotted spoon, remove the chicken and put to one side.

5 Add the potatoes to the wok or pan and simmer for a further 30 minutes.

6 Return the chicken to the pan and heat through. Transfer to serving dishes and sprinkle with the fried shallots.

Stir-fried chicken with chilli jam

6 garlic cloves, peeled and finely
    chopped
1½ tablespoons Chilli Jam (see page 55)
500 g / 1 lb 2 oz skinless chicken breast
    fillets, cut into 2.5 cm / 1 inch slices
a handful of fresh basil leaves
vegetable oil, for frying
1 large, fresh red chilli, deseeded and
    finely chopped, to garnish

For the sauce

2 tablespoons oyster sauce
60 ml / 2½ fl oz coconut milk
2 teaspoons Thai fish sauce (nam pla)
½ teaspoon Demerara or palm sugar

1 Mix all the ingredients for the sauce in a small bowl and put to one side.

2 Heat some oil in a wok or heavy-based frying pan and stir-fry half the garlic until it is just turning golden.

3 Add half the chilli jam and stir-fry for another couple of minutes, then increase the heat, add half the chicken and stir-fry for another 2 or 3 minutes. Remove from the wok and keep warm. Repeat the process with the rest of the garlic, chilli jam and chicken.

4 Return all the chicken to the wok, add the sauce mixture and stir-fry for a few more seconds or until the chicken is cooked.

5 Stir in the basil leaves, garnish with the chopped chilli and serve.

Above *Red bird's eye chillies.*

Stir-fried chicken with crispy basil

500 g / 1 lb 2 oz skinless chicken breast
    fillets, cut into 2.5 cm / 1 inch strips

2 handfuls of fresh basil leaves

2 tablespoons chicken stock

½ teaspoon Demerara or palm sugar

1 red pepper, deseeded and cut into
    strips

1 red onion, peeled, cut in half and sliced
    quite thickly

vegetable oil, for deep-frying

For the marinade

4 garlic cloves, peeled and finely
    chopped

4 small, dried red bird's eye chillies,
    crushed

2 tablespoons oyster sauce

1 tablespoon Thai fish sauce (nam pla)

1 Mix all the ingredients for the marinade in a bowl. Add the chicken strips and mix well, then cover and leave in the fridge for about 30 minutes.

2 Heat at least 5 cm / 2 inches of oil in a wok or heavy-based frying pan. Drop in two-thirds of the basil leaves and fry for about 30 seconds until they are crispy. Using a slotted spoon, remove from the wok and drain on kitchen paper, then set aside.

3 Throw this oil away, heat a small amount of fresh oil in the wok and stir-fry half the chicken over a high heat for 4–5 minutes, then remove and drain on kitchen paper. Stir-fry the remaining chicken, then return all the chicken to the wok.

4 Add the stock and sugar to the wok, then the red pepper and onion and stir-fry for another couple of minutes.

5 Stir in the fresh basil leaves, turn into a serving dish and garnish with the crispy basil leaves.

Thai desserts

Above left to right *A luscious array of rambutans and dragon fruit at Klong Toey Market. Rambutans are prickly beasts. The watermelon juice was very refreshing in the heat.*

Thai desserts

Sweet dreams, baby

In the land where one smile makes two, I am delighted to propose some outrageously sweet, sticky puddings (with only approximate measurements – I don't really know what a cup or a gram is!) that I made the Thai way, and for once, I do not support Shakespeare's diktat: 'A surfeit of the sweetest things to the stomach a certain loathing brings.'

Rice pudding with lychees

500 g / 1 lb 2 oz sticky (glutinous) rice
650 ml / 1 pint 2 fl oz jasmine water (this
   can be made by adding a few drops of
   jasmine essence to water)
500 g / 1 lb 2 oz Demerara, palm sugar or
   soft brown sugar
1 can lychees, drained
250 ml / 8½ fl oz coconut cream
½ teaspoon salt

1 Thoroughly wash the rice at least twice to remove any excess starch. Place in a pan with the jasmine water and bring to the boil, then reduce the heat and simmer, uncovered, until cooked through – about 15 minutes.

2 Add the sugar to the rice and cook until all the sugar has dissolved, then stir in the lychees. Remove from the heat.

3 Mix the coconut cream and salt in a saucepan. Gently bring to the boil, then remove from the heat.

4 Serve the rice and lychees in a bowl with the coconut cream poured over the top.

Fruit platter

1 small pineapple, peeled, eyes and core
   removed, and cut into chunks
1 galia melon, peeled, deseeded and cut
   into chunks
½ honeydew melon, peeled, deseeded
   and cut into chunks
8 fresh lychees, peeled, or canned
   lychees, drained
sprig of fresh mint, to garnish

For the syrup
200 g / 7 oz white caster sugar
500 ml / 17 fl oz water
2 tablespoons lime juice
5 cm / 2 inch strip lime rind

1 To make the syrup, put the sugar and water in a saucepan and stir over a medium heat until the sugar has fully dissolved, then add the lime juice and rind and bring to the boil. Boil without stirring for 10 minutes until you have a syrup. Remove the rind from the pan and set the mixture aside to cool.

2 Place all the prepared fruit in a large serving bowl and leave in the fridge for at least 1 hour to chill.

3 Just before serving, pour the syrup over the fruit and fold through so that all the fruit is coated. Garnish with a sprig of mint.

Spicy coconut custard

2 cinnamon sticks

1 teaspoon ground nutmeg

2 teaspoons whole cloves

300 ml / 10 fl oz double cream

250 ml / 8½ fl oz water

270 ml / 9 fl oz coconut milk

150 g / 5 oz Demerara or palm sugar

3 whole eggs and 2 egg yolks, beaten
    together in a large bowl

1 Preheat the oven to 160ºC / 325ºF / gas mark 3.

2 Put the spices, cream and water in a medium-sized pan and bring up to simmering point. Reduce the heat to low and leave for 5 minutes to infuse the spices.

3 Add the coconut milk and sugar and put on a low heat, stirring until the sugar has dissolved. Cool slightly.

4 Pour this mixture over the beaten eggs and egg yolks, mix well and then strain into a jug, discarding the spices.

5 Pour the mixture into 8 ramekins. Place the ramekins in a roasting pan and pour boiling water into the pan so that it comes halfway up the sides of the dishes.

6 Bake in the oven for 40–45 minutes. To check if the custards are cooked, insert a sharp knife into the middle of the custard. If it comes out clean, the custards are cooked. Serve hot or cold.

Pumpkin custard

1 small pumpkin

4 eggs

100 g / 3½ oz Demerara or palm sugar

120 ml / 4 fl oz coconut cream

1 Cut a 'lid' out of the top of the pumpkin and scoop out the seeds and membrane inside, leaving the flesh intact.

2 Break the eggs into a mixing bowl, add the sugar and coconut cream and whisk together until all the sugar has dissolved.

3 Sit the scooped-out pumpkin in a bowl to keep it upright and pour in the custard mixture. Place the bowl in a bamboo steamer set over a pan of boiling water with the pumpkin 'lid' to the side of the steamer. Steam for 30–40 minutes, or until the custard is set.

4 Allow to cool, then bring to the table with the pumpkin lid on and cut into wedges to serve.

Candied bananas (1)

4 firm bananas, peeled and cut into
    5 cm / 2 inch lengths
500 ml / 17 fl oz water mixed with juice of
    1 lime
500 ml / 17 fl oz water mixed with
    450 g / 1 lb Demerara, palm or soft
    brown sugar

1 Soak the bananas in the lime water for 30 minutes, then drain and rinse in clear water. Drain again and dry.

2 Put the sugared water in a wok or heavy-based, deep-sided frying pan and cook over a medium heat until the sugar has dissolved.

3 Bring to the boil and drop in the bananas, then boil, stirring occasionally to coat the bananas, until the syrup is thick and the bananas have turned pale red.

4 Remove from the pan and arrange on a serving dish. Serve warm or cold.

Candied bananas (2)

500 ml / 17 fl oz water mixed with
    450 g / 1 lb Demerara, palm or soft
    brown sugar
6 firm bananas, peeled and cut into
    5 cm / 2 inch pieces
250 ml / 8½ fl oz coconut cream
a pinch of salt

1 Put the sugared water in a pan and heat, stirring, until the sugar has dissolved, then bring to the boil and boil until you have a thick syrup.

2 Place the bananas in the syrup and boil over a medium heat for about 8 minutes, turning occasionally, until the bananas are soft and glossy. Place the bananas in a serving dish.

3 Mix the coconut cream and salt in a small pan and bring to the boil, then remove from the heat and allow to cool.

4 Serve the bananas with the cooled coconut cream drizzled over the top.

Deep-fried banana

4 ripe bananas
vegetable oil, for deep-frying

For the batter
115 g/4 oz self-raising flour
¼ teaspoon salt
25 g/1 oz grated coconut
2 tablespoons sesame seeds
2 teaspoons Demerara, palm or soft
    brown sugar
½ teaspoon baking powder
350 ml/12 fl oz water

1 Place all the ingredients for the batter into a bowl and whisk until you have a batter. Leave to rest for about 20 minutes.

2 Peel the bananas and cut in half lengthways, then cut into about 5 cm/2 inch lengths.

3 Preheat the oven to 150°C/300°F/gas mark 2. Heat enough oil for deep-frying (about 5 cm/2 inches) in a wok or pan, over a medium heat, but do not let the oil get too hot.

4 Dip the banana pieces into the batter and gently lower about 4 or 5 pieces at a time into the hot oil so that they sizzle. When they are golden brown, lift out with a slotted spoon, drain on kitchen paper, put on a dish and keep warm in the oven.

5 Continue this process until all the banana is cooked. Serve hot.

Banana in coconut milk

10 ripe bananas
750 ml/1¼ pints coconut milk
150 g/5 oz Demerara, palm or soft
    brown sugar
a pinch of salt
120 ml/4 fl oz coconut cream

1 Peel the bananas, cut in half lengthways, then cut the lengths in half to get 4 pieces.

2 Pour the coconut milk into a pan and cook over a medium heat until it boils. Add the bananas and cook for about 5 minutes until soft.

3 Stir in the sugar and salt and cook until the sugar has dissolved, then add the coconut cream and cook gently to heat through.

4 Remove from the heat, pour into a bowl and serve warm.

Pumpkin in coconut milk

1 litre/1¾ pints water
juice of 1 lime
1 kg/2¼ lb ripe pumpkin, deseeded,
    and cut into 1 x 1.5 cm/½ x ¾ inch
    chunks
1 litre/1¾ pints coconut milk
150 g/5 oz white caster sugar
a pinch of salt
250 ml/8½ fl oz coconut cream

1 Put the water and lime juice in a large bowl and drop in the pumpkin chunks. Leave to soak for 30 minutes.

2 Mix the coconut milk, sugar and salt in a pan and cook over a medium heat, stirring, until the sugar has dissolved, then bring to the boil.

3 Drain the pumpkin and add to the boiling coconut milk in the pan, then reduce the heat and simmer for about 15 minutes, or until the pumpkin is cooked.

4 Pour in the coconut cream and bring back to the boil. Turn off the heat and pour into a bowl to cool. Serve hot or cold.

Sweet potato in ginger syrup

1 litre/1¾ pints water
500 g/1 lb 2 oz sweet potato, peeled and
    cut into bite-sized chunks
1 cm/½ inch piece fresh root ginger,
    peeled and cut into slices
150 g/5 oz Demerara or palm sugar

1 Bring the water to the boil in a large pan and drop in the potato chunks. Add the ginger and boil for about 15 minutes until the potato is cooked through.

2 Add the sugar and allow it to dissolve completely, then remove from the heat and serve hot.

Right *Palm sugar.*

Sweet water chestnuts with coconut cream and syrup

10 drops of red food colouring
325 ml / 11 fl oz water
2 x 225 g cans water chestnuts, drained
    and cut into small pieces
150 g / 5 oz tapioca flour
250 g / 9 oz Demerara, palm or soft
    brown sugar
185 ml / 6½ fl oz coconut cream
a pinch of salt
crushed ice, to serve

1 Mix the red food colouring with 75 ml / 3 fl oz of the water in a bowl. Drop in the pieces of water chestnut and leave until they turn pink (10–15 minutes), then drain and leave to dry.

2 Sift the tapioca flour into a bowl and drop in the pink water chestnuts, rolling them around to coat them in the flour, then lift them out and shake off any excess flour.

3 Bring a saucepan of water up to the boil, add half the water chestnuts and cook for a couple of minutes. Using a slotted spoon, transfer them straight into a bowl of iced water to stop the cooking process. Repeat this with the remaining water chestnuts. When the water chestnuts are cold, drain them and set aside.

4 Heat the remaining measured water in a small pan, add the sugar and heat until the mixture boils, stirring all the time until the sugar has dissolved. Boil for 8–10 minutes until you have a thick syrup.

5 Put the coconut cream and salt in a pan over a low heat and cook for a couple of minutes until creamy.

6 To serve, divide the pink water chestnuts into individual serving bowls, drizzle over a little of the sugar syrup and a little of the coconut cream and top with crushed ice.

Sticky rice with mango

4 large ripe mangoes
1 quantity of room temperature steamed
    Sticky Coconut Rice (see page 63)
175 ml / 6 fl oz coconut cream mixed with
    a pinch of salt

1 Peel the mangoes and cut the two 'cheeks' off either side of the large stone. Slice them lengthways into 4 or 5 pieces.

2 Place a portion of the sticky rice on a serving dish, arrange the mango slices on the top and drizzle over the coconut cream.

Black glutinous rice with fresh coconut

500 g/1 lb 2 oz black glutinous (sticky)
    rice
1 litre/1¾ pints fresh coconut juice
300 g/11 oz Demerara, palm or soft
    brown sugar
300 g/11 oz fresh, grated coconut
250 ml/8½ fl oz coconut cream
a pinch of salt

1 Thoroughly wash the rice at least twice, then place in a saucepan with the coconut juice. Bring to the boil, then reduce the heat and simmer until the rice has cooked through and has started to split – this will take 12–15 minutes depending on the quality of your rice.

2 Add the sugar and simmer until the sugar has dissolved.

3 Add the fresh coconut and stir well, then bring to the boil one more time and turn off the heat.

4 Put the coconut cream and salt in a small pan over a low heat and gently heat through.

5 To serve, spoon the rice into serving dishes and top with the coconut cream.

Rice balls with fresh coconut

For the tapioca balls
250 g/9 oz tapioca
120 ml/4 fl oz very hot water
75 ml/2½ fl oz coconut cream
100 g/3½ oz fresh, grated coconut

For the coconut milk
500 ml/17 fl oz coconut milk
150 g/5 oz Demerara, palm or soft
    brown sugar
1 tablespoon rice flour
a pinch of salt
2 pandanus leaves (see page 104), cut
    into 2.5 cm/1 inch pieces, or a few
    drops of vanilla extract

1 To make the coconut milk, mix the coconut milk, sugar, rice flour and salt in a saucepan and bring to the boil. Once the mixture is boiling add the pandanus leaves or vanilla extract. When the mixture starts to give off the fragrance of the leaves, take off the heat and strain into a serving bowl, discarding the leaves.

2 In a large bowl, mix the tapioca with the hot water and stir thoroughly. Allow to cool slightly.

3 Add the coconut cream to the tapioca and knead until soft, then set aside to cool for 30 minutes.

4 When the tapioca mixture is cool, shape into small balls, about 1 cm/½ inch in diameter. Drop into boiling water and boil until they float to the surface, then remove them from the pan and drop them into the coconut milk.

5 Garnish with fresh, grated coconut.

Mango sorbet

3 ripe mangoes, peeled and flesh cut
   away from the stone
150 g/5 oz Demerara or palm sugar
185 ml/6½ fl oz water
juice and zest of 1 lime

1 Chop the mango flesh into small pieces.

2 Put the sugar and water in a saucepan and bring to
the boil, then reduce the heat and simmer until the liquid
has reduced by half. Set aside and allow to cool slightly.

3 Using a food processor, pour in the sugar syrup, mango,
lime juice and zest and whiz until very smooth. Pour into
a plastic container and put in the freezer, whisking at
least two or three times during the freezing process to
break down the ice crystals. Alternatively, if you have an
ice-cream maker, use that, following the instructions.

4 Store in the freezer until required.

Coconut ice cream

400 ml/14 fl oz coconut milk
250 ml/8½ fl oz double cream
2 whole eggs plus 4 egg yolks
160 g/5½ oz white caster sugar
a pinch of salt

1 Place the coconut milk and cream in a saucepan and
stir over a low heat for about 3 minutes, but do not boil.
Remove from the heat, cover and keep warm over a bowl
of hot water.

2 Put the eggs, egg yolks, sugar and salt in a bowl and
whisk energetically (preferably with an electric whisk) for
about 3 minutes until the mixture is light and fluffy.

3 Place the bowl over a pan of simmering water and
continue to whisk, slowly adding the coconut mixture
until the custard thickens, about 10 minutes in all.
Remove the custard from the heat and allow to cool.

4 If you have an ice-cream maker, pour the cooled mixture
into that and follow the instructions on the machine.
If not, pour the custard into a plastic bowl or container
and place in the freezer. Whisk at least twice while the ice
cream is setting to break up any ice crystals. You can
then store the ice cream in the freezer until it is needed.

Index